NICOLE MALLALIEU

the SAVVY
Seamstress

An Illustrated Guide to
Customizing Your Favorite Patterns

stashBOOKS®

an imprint of C&T Publishing

Publisher:
Amy Marson

Creative Director:
Gailen Runge

Editor: Liz Aneloski

Technical Editor:
Alison M. Schmidt

Cover/Book Design:
Page + Pixel

Production
Coordinators:
Joe Edge and
Tim Manibusan

Production Editor:
Jennifer Warren

Illustrators:
Nicole Mallalieu and
Aliza Shalit

Photo Assistant:
Mai Yong Vang

Instructional photography by Nicole Mallalieu. Style photography by Lucy Glover and garment detail photography by Diane Pedersen of C&T Publishing, Inc., unless otherwise noted.

Published by Stash Books, an imprint of C&T Publishing, Inc., P.O. Box 1456, Lafayette, CA 94549

Library of Congress Cataloging-in-Publication Data

Names: Mallalieu, Nicole Claire, 1968- author.

Title: The savvy seamstress : an illustrated guide to customizing your favorite patterns / Nicole Mallalieu.

Description: Lafayette, CA : C&T Publishing, Inc., [2017] | Includes bibliographical references and index.

Identifiers: LCCN 2017013883 | ISBN 9781617453113 (soft cover)

Subjects: LCSH: Dressmaking--Pattern design. | Clothing and dress measurements.

Classification: LCC TT520 .M245 2017 | DDC 646.4--dc23

LC record available at https://lccn.loc.gov/2017013883

Printed in the USA

10 9 8 7 6 5 4 3 2 1

INTRODUCTION

I've always been a garment maker. I was a child who made doll clothes, a teenager who was obsessed with sewing my own clothes, a fashion student, a designer pattern maker, and then a pattern designer and teacher. I still make most of my own wardrobe, often using the same small selection of basic patterns that I adapt with different fabrics and design details. I'm lucky to have a strong background in pattern making and sewing, but, as a teacher, I know that even relative beginners can learn to make the most of their pattern stash this way.

When I began teaching at a fashion college, most of the pattern-making and industrial sewing resources I found were pitched at a higher skill level than my students had. I had to break down the processes into small, achievable steps so my students could make the garments they designed. It occurred to me that the average home dressmaker could benefit from the same information.

By learning how to make a few key design alterations, you can keep transforming your favorite patterns—adding or removing collars and pockets, changing neckline shapes, and swapping a zippered back for a button front, a waistband for a facing, or vice versa. The variations are endless. I hope that this book gives you the inspiration and the confidence to try some of these changes, and that you are amazed by what you can achieve.

Contents

The SAVVY Seamstress

How to Use This Book

This book will not show you how to create or customize a pattern to fit your particular shape—that's a completely different area of pattern making, and there are already many helpful books and resources dedicated to it. The beginning point here is that you have a garment pattern that is the finished shape and fit that you want. You then need to decide on the features you'd like to add or change on it.

To be ready to start making alterations to a pattern, you need to have some basic sewing skills already, so you'll see that unless I have a particular tip or method to make something easier, I haven't wasted pages on the standard how-to-sew information. Instead, I've focused on detailed instructions, combining production-style industrial sewing methods with tricks and gadgets from the domestic-sewing sphere to help you gain speed and confidence in your sewing and give your new handmade wardrobe a professional finish.

Before you begin, read Pattern-Making Basics (page 16) to learn the fundamental terminology and processes that will be repeated throughout the book. Even if you have some pattern-making experience, it's important to understand the processes as they are defined and intended to be used in the instructions that follow.

I also recommend investing in a few simple pattern-making and sewing tools as described in Tools of the Trade (page 9). Successful sewing relies on accurate pattern making and cutting, and having the right equipment will make the journey easier and more rewarding than if you try to rely on low-tech workarounds.

For each design detail, I will guide you through the pattern adjustment and then on to the sewing instructions. Begin by working on simple garment shapes and changing one small detail at a time on your favorite pattern—fitting these instructions in around the original pattern instructions—and you'll begin to see how details can be interchanged on almost all patterns.

Some techniques depend upon the use of another—for example, a zippered opening needs a facing or waistband, and a collar needs a button facing or placket. Because of the interchangeability of all these components, the techniques are grouped into chapters so you can mix and match the pieces to create endless garment designs. It's best to sketch (or think through) your design first and then bookmark the various related instructions before you begin to make patterns or sew.

Make a test garment (a *toile* or *muslin*) before trying any new patterns or adjustments in final fabric. Traditionally, a basic plain-weave cloth (called *muslin* in the United States and *calico* elsewhere) is used for this, but you can make your test garment in any old not-particularly-precious fabric that has a similar weight, stretch, or drape to your final fabric. You can wear the test garment if it works and recycle it if it doesn't. Sometimes my test garments become the most worn items in my wardrobe; other times, they are recycled into new test garments or craft projects.

Tips • *If you're just branching out past the basics of dress-making, begin with simple shapes (children's wear is ideal) and with one of the "basic" techniques. You will gain confidence and skills to move forward.*

• *As you follow the pattern-making instructions, note the name of each pattern piece and how it relates to the finished garment (for example, which is top or bottom and what it connects to). Before you sew, note the right and wrong sides of the fabric, visualizing how it will sit on the finished garment. As this practice becomes habit, garment construction will become more intuitive and instructions easier to follow.*

• *Much of pattern making is estimating shapes and measurements. If you're unsure what size or shape to make a new garment component, use an existing garment as a guide. Never overthink the first estimation of any new shape or measurement. Try it and test it; then tweak the pattern accordingly. An experienced pattern maker develops an eye for getting it right only after years of tweaking nearly right first guesses.*

• *My biggest tip for using this book is to aim for absolute accuracy in your measuring, marking, cutting, and sewing—you'll save a lot of time unpicking or fudging things together. I believe that if you aim for absolute accuracy, what you achieve will be near enough. (Don't obsess over minor slipups.) You'll develop the habit of being careful where it matters. If you go in with a slap-dash attitude, your work will never improve.*

Now ... let's get started!

Tools of the Trade

Accuracy is important in pattern making, and the right tools will help you achieve this accuracy effortlessly.

PATTERN PAPER

To alter or draft new pattern pieces, you'll need paper that is light enough for tracing and heavy enough to lie flat, hold a firm crease, and withstand friction from an eraser. Some people use light nonwoven interfacing or similar products, but real paper works best for me. About 50 gsm is perfect—it's a little lighter than your average computer printer paper. It's best if you can see the lines that you draw from both sides of the paper and trace easily from one layer to another.

My favorite pattern-making paper is white, semiopaque, and printed with a grid of dots and crosses. It's known as dot-and-cross paper or marker paper, and its markings enable you to align pattern pieces to a grid, so you know when things are square and where the straight of grain and bias fall on any part of the pattern.

You can usually buy large rolls of pattern-making paper from paper mills, packaging warehouses, or fashion industry suppliers. You might find a sewing supplies store selling it in quantities that suit your needs and budget. Otherwise, a large layout-pad sketchbook, baking parchment, or tracing paper will suffice.

Tip *When altering or drafting patterns on semiopaque pattern paper, place one or two layers of paper beneath the one that you are working on. This increases the whiteness of the paper and the contrast of the lines that you draw, and makes it easier to trace lines through to new layers of paper.*

PENCILS

For pattern making, you need to use a sharp pencil. Thick lines create inaccuracies in seamlines and seam allowances, and small inaccuracies can add up to garment pieces that do not fit together as they should. Either have a pencil sharpener on hand or use a mechanical pencil.

RULERS

A clear plastic ruler and some sort of set square are necessary for making patterns. You need to rule construction lines and seam allowances, and you will need to use rulers to trace patterns from one piece of paper to the next. If possible, it's worth investing in rulers that are specifically designed for the task.

Dressmaker's Square Ruler

This long (24″ [60 cm]) ruler has two straight edges with a 90° corner and a curved edge designed to match many of the body's curves. A dressmaker's square helps you quickly draw long lines, right angles, and accurate curves on your patterns. If you can, buy one with seam allowance lines on the straight edges and around the hip curve. That feature will save you time and make all your patterns very accurate.

Curved Rulers

There are many different types of curved rulers, including vary form curve, French curve, and hip curve, which will help you draw smooth curves for necklines, armholes, waists, and hips. The most useful curved rulers are clear and have seam allowance lines.

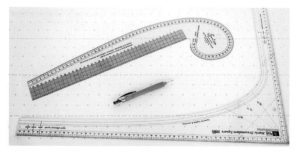

Dot-and-cross paper, dressmaker's square, and French curve. Note the seam allowance on the edges of both rulers.

Pattern-Maker's Ruler

There are also compact pattern-making rulers (such as the PatternMaster ruler) that include a short straight edge with a right angle and several curves on the inside edges, all with seam allowance markings. These rulers have all you need except a very long edge, so you may prefer to use one of these in combination with a long straight ruler.

Quilting Ruler

This isn't a standard pattern-making tool, but I use my 6″ × 24″ quilting ruler all the time. It allows me to accurately measure and rule parallel lines, and I also use it when I'm cutting out fabric pieces with a rotary cutter.

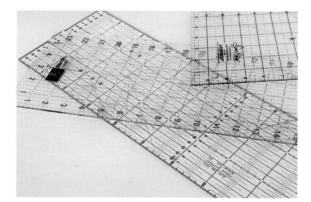

Quilting rulers

CUTTING EQUIPMENT

Successful sewing relies on the preparation you undertake in the pattern-making and cutting stages, so it's important to have the right cutting tools.

Scissors

Sharp dressmaking scissors are essential. You will struggle to cut with any speed or accuracy with cheap, badly weighted, wonky-bladed, or blunt scissors. The whole task will be much less satisfying than it should be. I advise investing in one pair of quality dressmaking scissors, which will last you a lifetime if you take care of them.

Pinking shears, appliqué scissors, and dressmaking scissors

Pinking shears are scissors that cut a zigzag line. They are used to trim ("pink") the edges of seam allowances to limit fraying (in lieu of serging) and to reduce bulk on seam allowances when curved edges are sewn together.

To trim and clip seam allowances, use a small pair of very sharp, pointy scissors. Some like embroidery scissors. I prefer to use appliqué or "duckbill" scissors, which have a sharp point on one blade and a flat half-moon shape on the other. They are designed to hold back one fabric layer while you snip away the top layer, but I use them for absolutely all my small trimming and clipping, as they are sharp and ergonomic.

Use reasonably sharp scissors with straight blades, even when you cut paper. For patterns to remain accurate, you need to cut exactly along a fine pencil line. Cheap scissors (or scissors with damaged blades) make this difficult.

Rotary Cutters

Using a rotary cutter is the fastest and most accurate way to cut out a pattern on fabric, but it takes practice to master the technique. A large rotary cutter is best for cutting long, straight edges, and smaller blades are easiest for cutting around curves. Use a self-healing cutting mat to protect your table.

Place each pattern piece on the fabric and the quilting ruler on top. To ensure that the ruler doesn't slip, the table needs to be at a height where your elbow and shoulder can be in a straight line above your hand as you press the ruler onto the fabric, usually from a standing position. Use the quilting ruler as a guide as you cut the first edge of the pattern. Realign the ruler to the next edge—checking that the pattern piece has not moved—and cut the next edge. Repeat this all the way around the pattern. Cutting curves involves moving the ruler around the curve as you cut in a continuous line.

A rotary point cutter is a fixed ⅓-circle used to cut into points that can't be cut accurately with a rotary blade. They are excellent for cutting nicks at the notch points on patterns. A sharp craft knife (art scalpel) can often be used for the same purpose.

Rotary blades and point cutter

PRESSING EQUIPMENT

A good iron makes a huge difference in the finish of any garment. Pressing throughout the sewing process is important to make sure everything ends up where it needs to be, and a powerful shot of steam helps. And if things go awry, a good steamy press can hide a multitude of sins on a finished garment.

A sturdy ironing board is a necessity. You will also find a sleeve board—which is like a mini-ironing board—enormously useful. A pressing ham, a sleeve roll, and a pressing cloth (or a sturdy foldable cloth such as cotton moleskin or well-washed heavy denim) make it easy to press into garment nooks and crannies. A selection of wooden tools help when small details need to be pressed with high pressure, as the ironing board can have too much give. You can use professional point pressers, rods, and clapper boards or simply improvise with things like dowels, wooden spoons, rulers, and blocks.

An ironing press might be useful if you are using a lot of interfacing, although you'll need space to store it and table space to use it. A press allows you to fuse large areas of interfacing smoothly, cutting preparation time drastically. Since you don't need the steam function for fusing interfacing, you may be able to pick up an older second-hand model relatively cheaply.

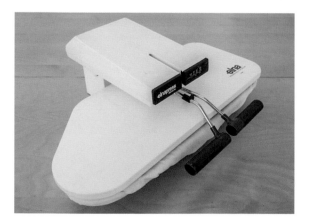

SEWING MACHINE AND PRESSER FEET

Sewing Machine

You don't need a fancy sewing machine to sew garments, just something with a good straight stitch, a variable zigzag, and an easy buttonhole function.

If you're looking for bells and whistles on a sewing machine, my top picks would be an easy automatic buttonhole, a needle-up/needle-down setting, and the option to use a knee-lift bar for the presser foot. The needle-up/needle-down function means that you can stop, start, or pivot your stitches with accuracy, and the knee-lift gives you maximum control over the presser foot grip on the fabric, allowing you to manage fiddly manipulations without having to take your hands off your work. (And in recent middle-aged years, I've come to love my needle threader!)

Presser Feet

A new sewing machine usually comes with a set of presser feet, and it's worth getting to know what each of these is designed to do. Some feet are not supplied with the machine and need to be purchased separately. These are the feet I wouldn't be without:

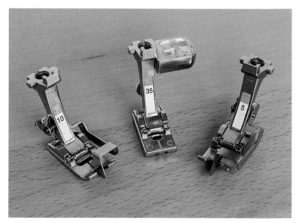

From left to right: edge-stitch foot, invisible zipper foot, and blind hem foot

NARROW OR SLIDING ZIPPER FOOT

A foot that can be set to sit on one side or the other of the needle is necessary for inserting zippers and for sewing into other awkward spaces. The narrower the foot is (the less bulk of metal directly in front of or behind the needle), the less likely it is to bump into the zipper pull or cause other problems.

A selection of narrow or sliding zipper feet

INVISIBLE ZIPPER FOOT

It's a breeze to insert an invisible zipper with the correct foot and pretty hard to do it without. Once you get the knack of invisible zippers, you will be using them as much as possible.

The bottom of an invisible zipper foot has two grooves and a small needle hole.

An invisible zipper foot uncurls the zipper chain as the machine stitches it in place.

BLIND HEM FOOT

Blind hemming is a quick alternative to hemming by hand. If you have a blind hem stitch on your sewing machine (a straight stitch with a left-pointing zigzag that acts as a catch stitch every few stitches), give it a try. The foot holds the hem in position, so the catch stitch isn't obvious on the right side of the fabric.

Blind hem foot

EDGESTITCHING FOOT

An edgestitching foot is a foot with a flange that sits in the seam. The needle can then be set at the required distance from the flange so the stitching is kept evenly spaced from the seam edge. Stitching neatly in the ditch of the seam is also made simple by setting the needle directly behind the flange. Not all machines have this foot, but it's worth checking to see if yours does or if there is a similar one that will do the job for you.

An edgestitching foot keeps topstitching evenly spaced from the edge of fabric.

Serger/Overlocker

A serger, or overlocker, is used to neaten the seam allowances on woven garments and to seam knit fabrics. You can get by without one, but these machines give a more professional finish to garments and are much faster than regular sewing machines. If you don't have a serger, use a zigzag stitch (width and length both set to around 3 [mm] on the sewing machine) to finish the edges of the seam allowances.

SEWING KIT ESSENTIALS

Pins

Pins are sometimes necessary, but they are often overused and can slow down the whole sewing process. Industrial sewing methods rely on notches and dots, which the machinist holds together as the fabric feeds through the machine. If you are more comfortable with pins, feel free to use them, but I encourage you to try to pin less and learn to use your hands—you will actually have more control that way.

I prefer to use weights to hold pattern pieces flat, and I cut with a rotary cutter, but you might like to use pins and scissors. If you pin pattern pieces to fabric, keep the pins at a right angle to the outer edge of the pattern, with the tips of the pins holding the edge of the paper against the fabric. Smooth the paper pattern and place pins about a handspan apart. Pin at an angle through the center of any corners. (Pins running parallel to the seamline curve the top and bottom layers of fabric at different rates, and this can cause inaccuracies in cutting.)

As with all sewing tools that depend on sharpness, don't waste your time or money on cheap, blunt pins; buy good-quality dressmaker pins.

Adhesives

Instead of pinning, I often use a fabric glue-stick pen or fusible tape (Vliesofix/Bondaweb T6 or Steam-A-Seam 2 tape) to hold things in place until they are sewn. Use only high-quality fabric adhesives that will not gum up your machine or needle, not office supplies.

NOTE *When I say to "fuse or pin" in the instructions, my recommendation is to use fusible tape instead of pins. Try it and you won't look back.*

Fusible ¼" tape and fabric glue-stick pen

Tailor's Awl / Stiletto

Anyone who has ever had a sewing lesson with me will have been introduced to the small marvel that is the tailor's awl. It is simply a spike with a handle on the end, and it's used to hold fiddly bits of fabric in place in front of the sewing machine needle, like a highly controllable pin. It is also great for making holes in things, and lots of other neat tricks. Get one.

Bias Tape Makers

These gadgets are the best! They are available in several widths and allow you to make neat bias binding in any fabric of your choosing (see Bias Binding, page 34). For garment making, the most commonly used widths are ½″ (12 mm) and ¾″ (18 mm).

Fabric Markers

Have an assortment of fabric marking tools at hand while you're cutting, sewing, or fitting garments. I love the accuracy of mechanical pencil–style markers. There are also air- and water-soluble felt-tip markers, various chalk pencils, wheels, tablets, and ballpoint pen markers. Experiment until you find what works best for you.

A dressmaker's tracing wheel is a spiky wheel tool that is used (with dressmaker's carbon or tracing paper under the pattern) to transfer lines through paper and onto fabric, marking curved darts, seamlines, and other design features onto the fabric pieces when notches and dots aren't enough.

A Hera marker is like a sharpened bone tool. It is used with a ruler to indent fine lines onto the surface of fabric to mark stitch lines on the right side of the fabric, which can be stitched over and then pressed out.

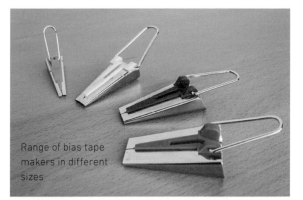

Range of bias tape makers in different sizes

Fabric markers

Dressmaker's tracing wheels

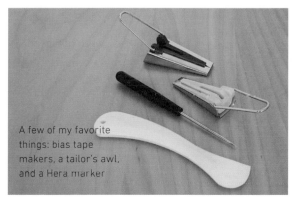

A few of my favorite things: bias tape makers, a tailor's awl, and a Hera marker

Pattern-Making Basics

Before you can alter a pattern piece, you need to completely understand what each piece does and what it connects to on the garment.

ANATOMY OF A PATTERN PIECE

Patterns are used to cut the fabric pieces that will be sewn together to make a garment. Before you can alter a pattern piece, you need to completely understand what each piece does and what it connects to on the garment. If you have no understanding of this, you need to construct the garment and take particular note of where seams connect each piece.

The key areas of patterns that will be mentioned throughout all the instructions also need to be understood, and I will use the following names and short-hand throughout the diagrams and notes.

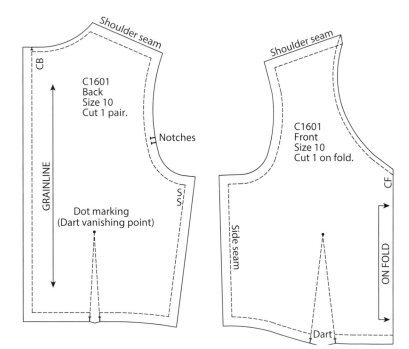

CF = CENTER FRONT

This is the vertical center through the front of the body that is marked on all drafts and patterns. It is used as a measuring point when designing a pattern, and it is a key notch point on any pattern piece that crosses the body horizontally, diagonally, or on a curve.

CB = CENTER BACK

The vertical centerline on the back of the body. Like the CF, this is a key measuring and notch point.

SS = SIDE SEAM

The side seam runs down the side of the body, directly from the center of the underarm. It's where the front and back pieces come together on most garments.

CUT ON FOLD / PLACE ON FOLD

"To cut on the fold" means that a pattern piece is designed to be placed against the folded edge of the fabric when cutting it out (see When to Cut on Fold, page 22). The symbol for this is a double-pointed arrow with a right angle at each end (the two arrow points on the fold line).

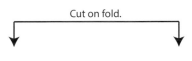

Cut on fold.

CUTTING INSTRUCTIONS

The pattern piece must always state how many of each piece to cut from fabric, interfacing, or lining.

Fabric is often folded selvage to selvage and both layers cut at once, which results in mirror pairs of anything marked "Cut 2" and allows for pieces to be "Cut on fold." When cutting unfolded fabric (for example, in an industrial setting, or if you need to cut so the pattern matches or cut from odd-shaped fabric scraps), any "Cut 2" pieces that are not purely symmetrical should be marked "Cut 1 pair." This means that the pattern piece must be cut once using each side of the pattern piece.

Notch

A notch is a registration mark on a pattern—drawn from the seamline through to the outer edge of the seam allowance—to show where pieces or seams of the garment connect. When the garment pieces are being cut, notches are marked on the fabric by a small snip (no longer than ⅛") or a chalk mark.

Grainline

The grain of the fabric refers to the direction of the yarns in the weave or knit of the cloth. The straight grain (warp) yarns run along the length of the fabric, parallel to the selvages, and are the strongest and straightest in the fabric.

Every pattern piece is marked with a grainline (a double-pointed arrow) to ensure that the fabric is cut with the grain in position to contribute to the best drape, surface appearance, and dimensional stability. When laying out pattern pieces for cutting, you align the grainline parallel to the selvages of the fabric (warp yarns).

Grain

NOTE *On a pattern for a knit garment, the double-pointed arrow might be used to denote the direction of the stretch in the fabric. This arrow will usually be labeled "Stretch."*

Dot Markings

Dots are also used to mark the placement of pockets, buttons, and the vanishing points of darts. In earlier times, these placement marks were transferred to the fabric with hand-stitched tailor's tacks, but this is completely unnecessary in most everyday sewing projects. If your fabric will not be spoiled by a chalk or fabric-marker dot as you cut out the garment pieces, you can mark directly through a tailor's awl hole on the pattern (see Tailor's Awl / Stiletto, page 15) onto the wrong side of the fabric.

To transfer the dot markings to the right side of the fabric for pocket placements and so on, simply poke pins through from the wrong side of the fabric.

SEAMLINES AND SEAM ALLOWANCE

The seam (or stitch) lines indicate the exact lines where the pieces of a garment are sewn together. When you are making or altering patterns, these are the key lines used to match the pattern pieces together, so it's important that they be clear and accurate. The seam allowance is the area between the seamline and the raw edge of the garment piece.

When a pattern piece is cut out in fabric, there are no lines to show you where to stitch; you know where the seamline is by knowing that it is the seam allowance width from the edge of the fabric. To be able to trust that this is correct, you need to be accurate through every step of the pattern-making and cutting processes.

If the seam allowance isn't correct to begin with, you will lose the ability to match two garment pieces together as they were designed to be. If your seam allowances are drawn accurately but cut sloppily or sewn with an incorrect seam allowance depth, you'll have the same problem.

Accuracy is vital where curves and angles are concerned—as is the case with most garment pieces. As a seam allowance is added to a convex seamline, the shape of the pattern piece gets larger toward the seam allowance edge, and on a concave edge it gets smaller (similarly with pointed or angled shapes). If the seam allowance is drawn, cut, or sewn too wide, too narrow, or unevenly, the line that will be perceived as the seamline on the fabric piece (for example, ½″ from the cut edge) will be larger or smaller than the actual seamline. As one garment piece is sewn to another, you will be trying to match two lines of completely different lengths.

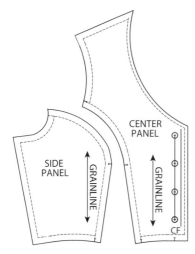

Correct seam allowances

Both red lines: 12¾″ (32.8 cm)

Seam allowances must be drawn, cut, and sewn accurately, or garment pieces will not fit together.

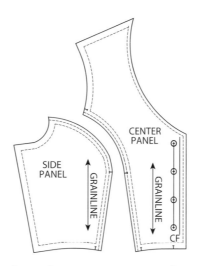

Seam allowance sewn too narrowly

Side panel line = 13⅛″ (33.5 cm)

Center panel = 12⅜″ (31.9 cm)

The side panel will appear ¾″ (2 cm) too big.

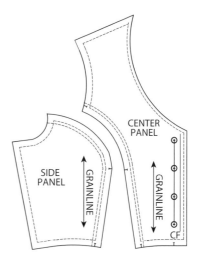

Seam allowance sewn too wide

Side panel line = 12½″ (32.2 cm)

Center panel = 13⅛″ (33.5 cm)

The center panel will appear ⅝″ (1.5 cm) too big.

On domestic sewing patterns, the standard seam allowance depth was traditionally ⅝″ (15 mm). Now it is often a more fabric-efficient ½″ or ⅜″ (12 mm or 10 mm). In the fashion industry, seam allowances are usually ⅜″ for exposed seams and ¼″ (6 mm) for enclosed or bagged-out edges (on facings, cuffs, collars, and so on), although some smaller producers still prefer to use ½″. Theater costumes are often made with 1″ (2.5 cm) seam allowances to allow for more alterations and ease. Whatever width you choose to use, it's important to keep it consistent and accurate throughout the entire process of pattern making, cutting, and sewing.

NOTE *I have used a standard of ½″ and ¼″ (12 mm and 6 mm) seams for this book because it is more common in the domestic sewing world, especially in the United States. You can change these measurements to your preferred seam allowance.*

DRAFTS AND PATTERNS

About Drafts

The draft is a copy of the pattern that acts as a map for the garment as you change the shape of the pattern pieces. It is drawn on a large, uncut piece of paper. Pattern pieces are then traced individually from the draft onto separate pieces of paper, and seam allowances are added to the pattern pieces, which are then cut out and used as templates to cut the fabric.

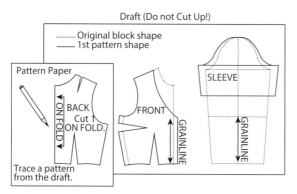

Patterns are traced from the draft onto separate pieces of paper.

Having the draft allows you to measure and match all the necessary lines without having to riffle through lots of separate pattern pieces every time you make a change, and it allows you to keep grainlines and notch positions accurate. It also works as a saved copy in case you accidentally lose or destroy one of the pattern pieces (believe me—it's easier than you think!) and can serve as a basic block from which to build new designs in the future.

With pattern making, you don't always get the result you want the first time, so the draft serves as a record of your changes as you develop the shapes and details for the new pattern. You make a toile/muslin (test garment)

and then make any necessary changes on the draft before tracing new pattern pieces. Sometimes you need to undo a change or find a halfway mark between two tested measurements, and the draft will help you do that. If there is a problem with the garment not fitting as it should, checking the pattern against the draft can often show where the problem lies.

Tips • The first step in most of these instructions is to make a draft copy of your pattern pieces. I recommend writing "Do not cut" on this copy immediately, as a reminder not to accidentally cut it out or make pattern pieces from it. You need to keep the draft whole.

• As you follow the instructions to make changes to the draft, always label the CF and CB. Also label the new lines that you draft so you remember what they are.

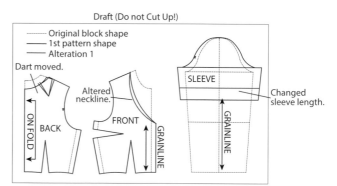

The draft is a map of all the changes made throughout the development of a new pattern design.

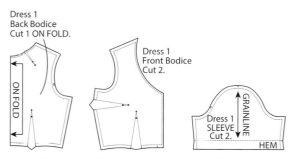

Dress 1
Back Bodice
Cut 1 ON FOLD.

ON FOLD

Dress 1
Front Bodice
Cut 2.

Dress 1
SLEEVE
Cut 2.

GRAINLINE

HEM

The pattern pieces have seam allowances added and include all the cutting instructions, grainlines, and markings needed to sew the garment.

Usually the draft is drawn *nett* (without seam allowances) so there is no confusion about where the seamlines are—you can measure each line accurately and see the exact shapes that will appear on the finished garment. It is much less confusing than making alterations on a jumble of individual pattern pieces with seam allowances in some places and not in others. When you trace the patterns from the altered draft, simply add seam allowances on all the outer edges of each pattern piece.

NOTES

• *The instructions in this book are written to accommodate all sewing patterns, including home-drafted and commercial patterns with and without seam allowances. To keep the instructions clear, all methods begin with making a draft copy of the pattern without seam allowances.*

• *For simple alterations, such as pockets, you may not need to remove the seam allowances (nor indeed make a full draft) from your pattern, but you must always know where the seamlines are. So it's a good idea to draw them on any patterns you want to alter.*

How to Make a Draft from an Existing Pattern

A draft copy is simply traced from the original pattern, following the seamlines instead of the outer edges of the seam allowances.

If seam allowances are included but not drawn on the pattern that you're using, you will need to find out what the seam allowance is and draw the stitch lines on the pattern pieces before you trace the draft copy. Follow the directions for adding seam allowances to a pattern piece (see How to Add Seam Allowances, page 26), but reverse the direction so you measure and draw the seamlines to the inside of the seam allowance edge. Then trace the nett shape onto a separate piece of paper to use as a draft copy.

Removing the seam allowance from an unmarked pattern

If your design idea involves removing a pattern's button extension or facing, trace the draft without it (tracing to the CF or CB only).

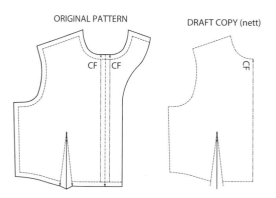

ORIGINAL PATTERN

DRAFT COPY (nett)

CF   CF

CF

WHEN TO CUT ON FOLD

When designing a symmetrical garment, we work on a draft that represents half the garment (CF to CB). If a particular pattern piece is symmetrical and we only need to "Cut 1" (for example, the front or back of a garment), that piece is marked with an "on fold" arrow along the centerline and no seam allowance along that edge. The piece is labeled "Cut 1 on fold." (You cannot have too much labeling where cutting is concerned.)

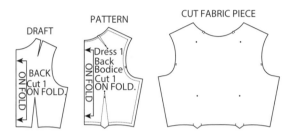

DRAFT   PATTERN   CUT FABRIC PIECE

Cutting fabric on the fold increases the margin for error on small symmetrical pieces that are "Cut 2." Unlike on larger pattern pieces, inaccuracies in laying out and cutting these pieces on the fold of fabric can form an obvious "banana bend" in the center or can mean that the two pieces are cut to slightly different sizes. For this reason, it is best to trace full patterns (not on the fold) before cutting the fabric.

A full pattern piece allows the two pieces to be cut from fabric at exactly the same size (often cutting two layers of fabric at the same time). It also means that pieces such as collars, collar stands, and yokes can be cut along the length-wise grain, as they traditionally should be, or on bias grain for decorative effect.

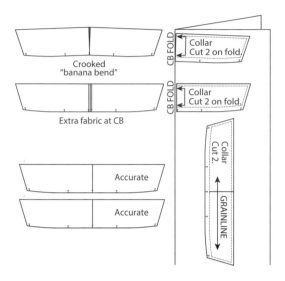

Crooked "banana bend"

Extra fabric at CB

Accurate

Accurate

Trace a Full Pattern from a Half-Draft

1. Cut a piece of pattern paper that is at least twice as wide as the draft, and fold it in half with a sharp crease. Place the crease line over the centerline of the draft and trace the pattern piece.

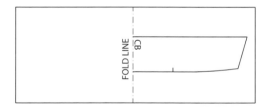

Tip   *Particularly on small pattern pieces, extend any line that meets the center-line at a right angle through to the other side of the fold. This will help keep the pattern square.*

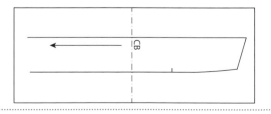

2. Add seam allowances, notches, and labels to the traced pattern piece.

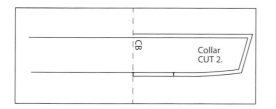

3. With the traced pattern to the outside, fold the paper along the crease line as shown, and align the extended right-angle lines (if any) with the traced pattern piece. Trace the pattern piece, including seam allowances and notches, onto the other side of the paper. The full pattern piece is now ready to cut out.

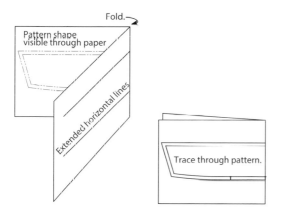

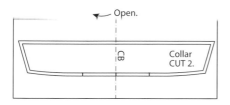

KEEPING THINGS SQUARE

Square alignment of structural lines is necessary to create the right shape and fit around the body with the correct grain of fabric, so a common direction in pattern-drafting instructions is to "square up," "square down," or "square across" from a given point on a line.

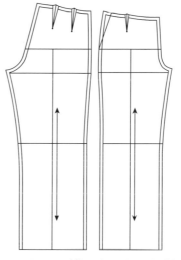

Square structural lines in pattern drafting

This means that you need to draw a line up, down, or across from that point at a right angle from the line. Use the lines and right-angled edge on a dressmaker's square or quilting ruler to do this.

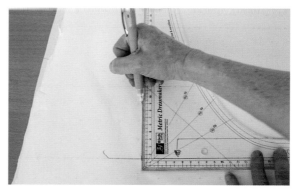

Squaring across from a vertical line

Pieces drafted as "On fold" at the CF or CB (unless the neckline is supposed to be a V-shape) need at least a tiny section of the center of the curve to be at a right angle from the centerline, or they can have unintended peaks or V's.

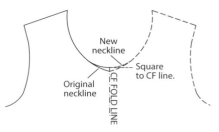

MOVING DARTS AND SEAMLINES

The most fundamental principle of pattern making is that once you have the pattern for the overall shape of a garment, you can move the seams and darts around to make new design lines and features. For example, you can turn a garment that opens at the front with buttons into one that has a plain front and zippered back opening (see Neckline Facing and Button Closure, page 75) or vice versa.

You can't take away from the positive space that the (nett) pattern makes, but you can cut it up and stick it together in different configurations. You can move or eliminate darts by opening up the pattern elsewhere to make facings (see Waistline Facings for Zippers, page 108), add yokes (see Classic Shirt Yokes, page 114), and add design lines.

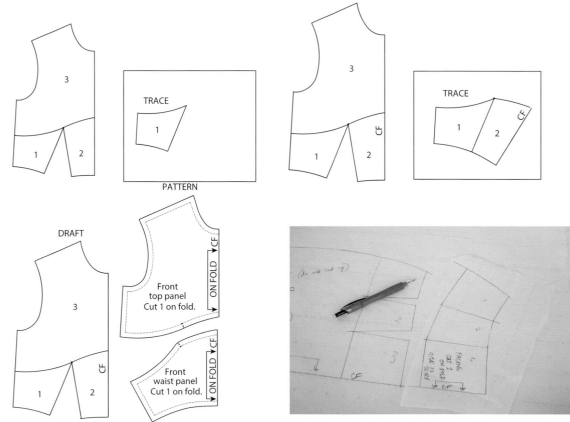

SLASH AND OPEN

Slashing and opening is the next fundamental principle of pattern making. It's the opposite of closing out a dart; you can open up any part of a pattern piece to add fit, flare, or gather. You can reshape sleeves, skirts, or indeed whole garments with extra fullness at the top, at the bottom, or all the way through. The possibilities and uses for this technique could fill another book. But if you understand the basic principle, it's worth experimenting with to make simple alterations to your patterns (see Classic Shirt Collar and Stand, Check and Tweak the Pattern, page 126) for a demonstration of the process in action.

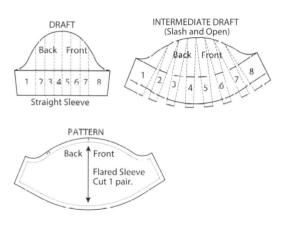

PROVING OR TRUEING A LINE

Once you have moved a dart or manipulated a pattern piece, you need to neaten the outer lines of the pattern and check that hemlines, necklines, and other seamlines flow smoothly over darts and seams. This is done by folding out any darts and aligning the seamlines on the draft and then smoothing out lines and curves with the appropriate (straight or curved) ruler.

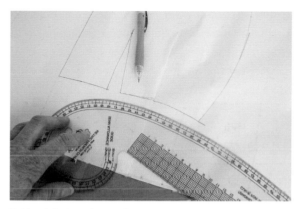

Fold out darts and smooth out curves on pattern pieces.

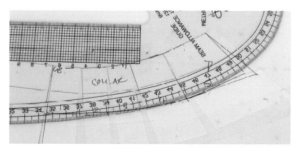

Neaten lines after pattern pieces have been manipulated.

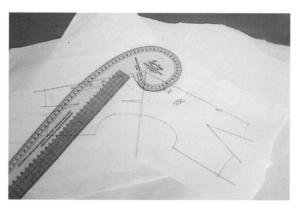

Smooth lines between adjoining pieces on a draft.

HOW TO ADD SEAM ALLOWANCES

Adding seam allowances is where having a proper pattern-making ruler comes into use; seam allowance depths marked as lines on the ruler make achieving accuracy a breeze. For straight lines, it's as easy as aligning the seam allowance line of the ruler with the stitch line on the pattern piece and ruling in the seam allowance around the outside.

To add seam allowances with curves, it helps if you have rulers with both convex and concave seam allowance marks. The curves change shape over the length of the rulers, and you need to match the seamline on your pattern to the part of the ruler that has the same shaped curve and trace around the edge. Sometimes you may be drawing only an inch or two of seam allowance at a time. Keep matching the next part of the seamline to a matching shape on the ruler, and add the seam allowances around all the curved edges.

If you don't have a curved seam-allowance ruler, you can use a quilting ruler or straight clear ruler to make lots of small straight lines at the seam allowance depth and then smooth these lines into a continuous line.

> *Tip* *On corners where the angle is acute (less than 90°), crossing over the seam allowances can make the point very long, which makes for inefficient cutting and can cause confusion when aligning seams at the sewing machine. When you draw in the seam allowances, extend them well beyond the corner of the pattern piece. Extend the stitch lines on both sides of the corner all the way through the seam allowances. Draw a line to connect the two intersections of stitch and seam-allowance lines. The line will be exactly the width of the seam allowance and will serve as a perfect guide for sewing the garment together. Cut off the point.*

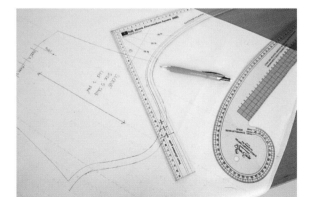

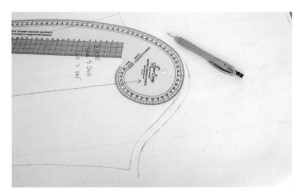

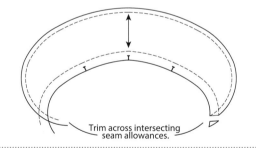

Trim across intersecting seam allowances.

DRAFTING EXTRA PATTERN PIECES

When you draft completely new pieces to add to a garment, vigilantly check your measurements. A collar has to fit onto a neckline, a cuff onto a sleeve. Always measure to the tiniest fraction of an inch or nearest millimeter, because even tiny fractions of inches can add up to make two garment pieces fit poorly together, creating puckers, stretching, and badly shaped garments.

To measure curved seamlines, stand your tape measure on its side and hold it inch by inch as you follow the drawn seamline with the edge of the tape.

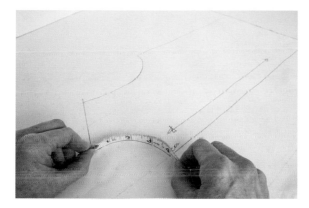

Keep the new draft with the garment draft, labeled with the garment name, piece name, grainline, and cutting instructions. These extra pieces usually look much the same and can easily be confused between different garment patterns, especially after a few weeks.

OVERWRAPS AND UNDERLAPS

When a piece of clothing closes with buttons or a zipper, there is usually an extension of fabric to hold the buttons, buttonholes, or zipper. For buttons, the buttonhole side is referred to as the overwrap and the button side is the underwrap; for lapped zippers, it's overlap and underlap.

If we look at women's garments, the overlap/wrap is conventionally the viewer's left over right; men have right over left. The direction continues all the way around the body for overlaps/wraps on side or back seams. General sewing directions when this is the case (as well as having right and wrong sides of fabric and "Whose left are we talking about?" questions) are less confusing if we simply refer to the overlap/wrap and underlap/wrap sides of the garment. Before you begin to make any alterations, you need to establish which side of the garment will be the overlap/wrap and which will be the underlap/wrap.

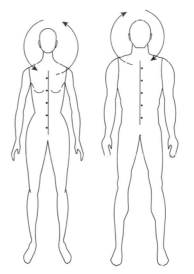

Sewing Techniques and Terminology

This section is pared back to address only the aspects that strictly apply to the techniques featured in this book.

I've assumed that if you are ready to begin tweaking patterns you have basic sewing skills, so this section is pared back to address only the aspects that strictly apply to the techniques featured in this book, where I can add a particular note, trick, or method I use. There are many, many other books and resources providing information on the very basics of sewing if you need more help.

SEAMS

A plain seam is usually sewn with a straight stitch setting of 2.5 (mm), backstitched at each end. The seam allowance is the buffer zone between the raw edges of the fabric and the seam. If left unfinished, the seam allowance can fray and the garment can fall apart. On unlined garments, all seam allowances must be finished with serged, zigzagged, pinked, or bound edges (see Attaching Binding to Seam-Allowance Edges, page 35), or enclosed in a French or felled seam (see Glossary, page 169).

EASING

Ease is needed in certain areas of a garment to create fullness, allowing for the shape and movement of the body. For example, ease is used in the cap of a set-in sleeve. This means that one seamline is longer than the other and is gently gathered up with an "ease stitch" sewn slightly to the inside of the seam allowance before the seam is sewn, so the two garment pieces match together without puckering.

To make an ease stitch, you can use a long stitch length and pull gently on the bobbin thread until the seam matches the other seam length. A faster production method, called *crimping* or *crowding*, is done with the same stitch length as the garment seams, with your finger held lightly against the back of the presser foot, bunching the fabric between your finger and the foot. This causes the fabric to crimp evenly in little stitch-length waves, which reduces the seamline length.

Crimping (or crowding)

For very small differences in seamline lengths, you don't even need the ease stitch. Simply place the smaller of the two pieces on top as you sew, and don't correct the action of the presser foot stretching the fabric forward as the feed dogs ease slightly more fabric to the underside. Often this action is enough to ease two different-length pieces together (for example, when sewing an upper collar to a slightly smaller undercollar).

STAYSTITCH

Staystitching is a line of (standard length) stitches, sewn slightly narrower than the seam allowance depth. Its purpose is to stabilize curved edges, such as necklines, armholes, and waistlines, so that the fabric does not distort or stretch during garment construction. The stitches stay in place even after the final seams are sewn.

My guilty sewing secret is that I often don't staystitch if the fabric is reasonably stable, but the best practice is to staystitch every neckline, armhole, or waistline (in any fabric) as soon as you cut the pieces or after you have joined shoulder and/or side seams.

There are now light fusible stay-tapes that do the work of stay stitching (with a little extra support). You simply iron it onto the seamline rather than stitching.

TOPSTITCHING AND EDGESTITCHING

Topstitching is any line of stitching that is sewn on the right side of the fabric. It is visible on the outside of the garment and is often used for decoration (sometimes with contrast or heavy topstitching thread) and to define the seams and edges of the garment. Topstitching creates structure along a seamline because it holds the extra bulk of the seam allowances directly against the outer fabric. It can also be used to attach parts of the garment (pockets, tabs, outer cuffs, collars, and so on) directly onto the right side of the fabric.

Edgestitching is a form of topstitching, but it is never any further from the seam than a generous 1/16″ (2 mm). Topstitching can be any distance from a seam or edge.

UNDERSTITCHING

Understitching is a form of edgestitching that occurs only on the inside of a garment. It creates a sharp, smooth line around a neckline, waist, or armhole, or anywhere a facing, lining, or underside needs to sit flat on the inside of a seamed edge.

How to Understitch a Facing

1. With the seam allowances folded to the facing side of the seam, turn the fabric to the right side. Do not press the seam.

2. Edgestitch along the facing a generous 1/16″ (2 mm) from the seamline, holding the seam allowances to the underside. Trim the excess seam allowance to 1/8″–1/4″ (3–5 mm).

3. Turn the facing to the inside of the garment and press the seam.

Where a facing has a corner (for example, a zipper or button facing), back the presser foot into the corner as far as you can without

trapping puckers of fabric underneath. Backstitch neatly and understitch your way around the facing, stopping and backstitching as close to the other corner as you can without the fabric puckering.

Facing

Tips
- *Use three fingers on each hand to open and flatten the seam in front of the needle as you sew, and use your thumb underneath to keep the seam allowances turned to the facing side.*

- *Use an edgestitching foot to keep understitching an even distance from the seam.*

BAR TACK

A bar tack is a small line of tight zigzag stitches (like on the side of a small buttonhole) that is used to secure areas of high wear and tear on garments. Set the machine to a narrow $\frac{1}{16}"-\frac{1}{8}"$ (2–3 mm) zigzag width and short stitch length (just above zero), and stitch for $\frac{3}{8}"-\frac{1}{2}"$ (10–12 mm). Test the stitch on a scrap of the fabric you are using before attempting it on your garment.

TURNINGS

When topstitching is used to hold fabrics together, the raw edge of the seam allowance needs to be turned to the wrong side of the fabric so it is enclosed between the layers of fabric. The folded area of the seam allowance is referred to as the *turning*. A hem that is folded up twice and topstitched in place is called a *double-turned hem*.

A common instruction is to "fold a turning" of a particular width, and this usually means to press it as well. With more practice, your ability to estimate measurements and press turnings will improve, but in the meantime, here are a few shortcuts that might help.

Stitched Guide Turning Trick

On a curved edge (such as a curved hemline on a shirt), you can mark the depth of the turning or hem by stitching a line a generous $\frac{1}{16}"$ (2 mm) narrower than the required turning in from the raw edge. For example, to turn a $\frac{1}{2}"$ (12 mm) hem, stitch a consistent width somewhere between $\frac{3}{8}"$ (10 mm) and $\frac{1}{2}"$ (12 mm) from the edge of the fabric all along the hemline.

Use this as a guide to press the hem in place, checking that the stitches are always visible just on the inside of the fold. To make a double-turned hem, turn the raw edges in to the crease at the bottom of the turning and press again.

Fusible Tape Turning Trick

You can use fusible tape (see Adhesives, page 14) that is the same width as the required turning (¼″ [3 mm], ⅜″ [10 mm], and so on) as a guide. Fuse the tape in place on the right side of the fabric along the edge that needs to be turned, keeping the tape straight and flush with the raw edge of the fabric. Don't remove the backing paper—use it as a guide to fold and press the turning sharply toward the wrong side of the fabric. When it is time to stitch the turned edge in place, remove the backing paper and press the turning to fuse it in place—no pins needed!

INTERFACING

Interfacing is a layer of fabric that is used inside the outer fabric of a garment to add support and structure to areas such as waistbands, facings, collars, cuffs, and plackets. Interfacing can be sewn in or fusible (ironed on).

How to Choose Interfacing

Tailoring and evening-wear construction require an understanding of a wide range of interfacings, but for general garment sewing you can get by with a limited range and knowledge, so don't stress too much about it. Try a few different types on some scrap fabric (or test garments) and you'll develop a feel for choosing the right one. A few rules of thumb can serve as a good guide:

- For lightweight fabric and small children's clothes, err on the side of lightweight (woven or nonwoven) interfacing. You don't want to make facings and cuffs too stiff. For heavier fabrics, choose heavier interfacing or it won't make much of a difference.

- For knit fabrics, use knit interfacing. For woven fabric, you can use either woven or nonwoven interfacing.

- For collars and cuffs on adult clothing, choose woven fusible interfacing that looks like lawn or poplin. It will give sturdy structure.

- Use light- to medium-weight (woven or nonwoven) interfacing on button stands and plackets. They don't need to be as stiff as collars.

- Use white or unbleached interfacing for light-colored fabrics and black interfacing for dark fabrics.

Fusing Interfacing

Refer to the manufacturer's instructions, if available, for the interfacing that you are using.

The adhesive is the shiny or grainy finish on one side of the fusible interfacing. Place this side against the wrong side of the fabric. If the interfacing is nonwoven, cover it with a pressing cloth to protect your iron.

Press firmly downward with the iron for five to ten seconds, and then lift the iron and move it to the next section and press, repeating this until you've fused the whole piece. Don't slide the iron as you press, or the interfacing may shift. An ironing press (page 12) makes this process a lot faster.

If the interfacing doesn't stick to the fabric, it needs more heat or pressure. If it bubbles and shrinks, you have used too much heat—rip it off and cut a new piece.

Sometimes interfacing is cut without seam allowances to reduce bulk and/or allow turnings to fold easily. If the interfacing needs to extend to the edge of the garment piece, block fusing (below) can make the process quicker and more accurate.

BLOCK FUSING INTERFACING

Roughly cut the interfacing a little larger than the pattern piece and fuse it to the wrong side of the uncut fabric; then use the pattern piece to cut through all the layers. This reduces distortion in cut pieces that need to fit together accurately.

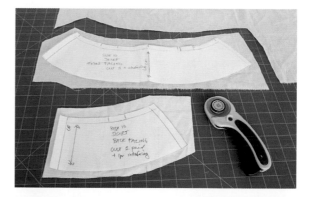

Block fusing: Fuse the interfacing to the fabric, place the pattern on the interfacing, and then cut out the piece.

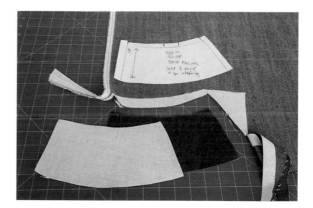

NOTE *Some people prefer to cut interfacing without a seam allowance for garment facings. I find that working around the distortion that happens when pieces are cut and fused separately takes more time and gives less satisfying results than block fusing. I block fuse, cut accurately, sew the seams accurately, and then peel the interfacing off the seam allowances and trim it to the seamline.*

BIAS BINDING

Binding is used as a high-end finish on seams (in lieu of overlocking or adding a lining) and a simple finish on necklines and armholes (in lieu of facings) and is also used decoratively. With a bias-tape maker, you can make bias binding in almost any light- to medium-weight fabric, which can be an exact match with the fabric of the garment or a contrasting fabric.

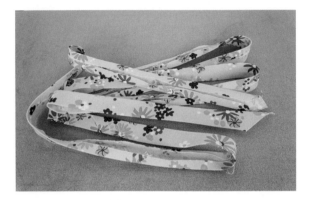

Rotary Cutting Bias Tape

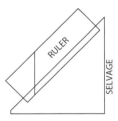 *To keep the fabric crisp and straight as you cut and feed it through the bias tape maker, especially if you're using unstable or fine fabric, spray laundry starch on the fabric before pressing. This also stabilizes the finished tape, making it easier to sew.*

1. Place the fabric on a rotary cutting mat. Find the bias (45°) line on your quilting ruler, and match this to the selvage on the fabric. Following the long edge of the ruler, cut a smooth, straight line using a rotary cutter.

This cut is on the true bias grain: 45° from the straight of grain.

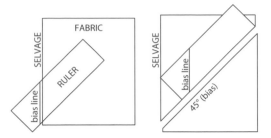

2. Use the ruler grid to measure the width of the bias tape that you need. The rule of thumb is to measure twice the width of the bias tape maker (for ¾″ [2 cm] bias tape, cut 1½″ [3.5–4 cm]). Align the measurement line with the bias-grain edge that you just cut.

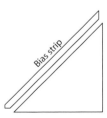

3. Use the edge of the ruler and a rotary cutter to cut the bias tape.

4. If needed, sew the bias tape strips together end to end to make longer strips. Follow the instructions in your bias-tape maker to join, fold, and press the bias strips.

Attaching Binding to Seam-Allowance Edges

1. Open one side of the bias binding and align its raw edge with the raw edge on the underside of the seam allowance. Stitch along the fold line of the bias tape.

2. Fold the unattached side of the binding around to the right side of the fabric. Align the unattached folded edge a generous ¹⁄₁₆″ (2 mm) over the first line of stitching. Press it in place (you can fuse or use a fabric glue stick to secure it).

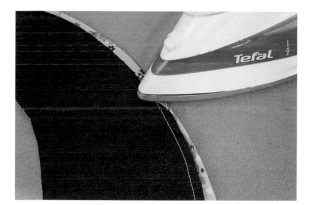

3. Edgestitch through all the layers of fabric to hold the binding in place, aiming to sew directly over the first stitch line.

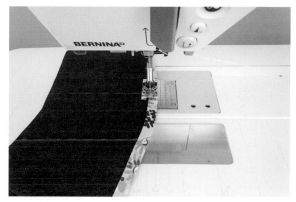

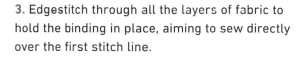 Use a tailor's awl to hold the edge of the tape in the correct position over the stitches. Place the point of the tailor's awl a generous ¹⁄₁₆″ (2 mm) from the folded edge, and then align that point with the stitches that attach the other side of the binding. "Walk" the awl in front of the needle, aligning the binding as you sew.

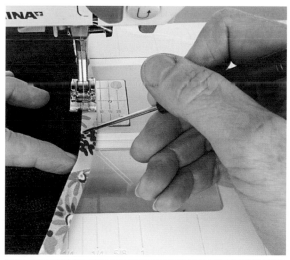

Pockets

Pockets can be functional or decorative, and changing the pocket detailing is probably the simplest addition or variation you can make to a pattern.

Inseam pocket

Patch pocket

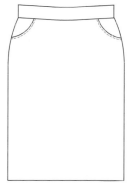

Inseam pocket with facing   Hip pocket

Placement is important for both ergonomic and design reasons. As you design the pattern, pin a paper pocket shape to a finished or test garment to check for comfort and ease of use. Also check that it is visually balanced with the proportions and shape of the garment.

PATCH POCKETS
Skill Level: Basic

Unlined patch pockets are used on jeans, shirts, and many other casual garments and are usually cut from the same fabric as the garment, unless a contrast color or print is used for decorative purposes.

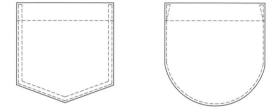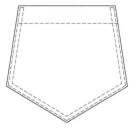

Prepare the Pattern and Fabric

1. Decide on the shape and placement of the pocket, and draw it on the draft of your garment in the position where you would like it to be. Mark a dot ⅛″ (3 mm) in from each top corner.

2. Place the pattern for the garment piece over the draft and align all the seamlines. Trace the pocket placement, including the dot placements. Write "Pocket placement" near the dots.

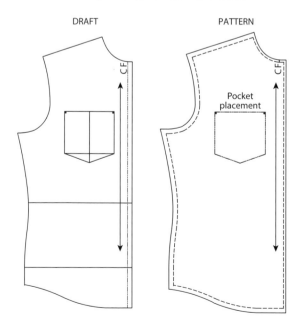

DRAFT   PATTERN

Pocket placement

3. Trace a pocket pattern from the draft, extending the horizontal line at the top of the pocket at least ½″ (12 mm) on each side. Rule a vertical grainline that is parallel to the grainline on the garment. Label and write the cutting instructions: "Cut 2" if there are 2 pockets on the garment and "Cut 1" for 1 pocket.

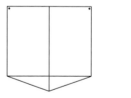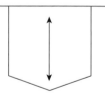

4. Add seam allowances around the sides and bottom edges of the pocket pattern. These seam allowances can be ¼″ (6 mm), ⅜″ (10 mm), or ½″ (12 mm), depending on your own preference or planned use of the fusible tape turning trick (page 32).

5. Add a 1¼″ (32 mm) allowance for the hem at the top edge. Cut out the pattern, and notch both ends of the line that extends through the side seam allowances, marking where to fold the hem turning at the top of the pocket.

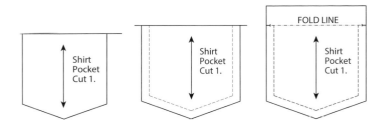

Sew the Patch Pocket

1. Transfer the dot markings for the pocket placement to the fabric garment piece.

2. Along the top edge of the pocket, press a ¼″ (6 mm) turning toward the wrong side of the fabric; then fold and press the hem allowance (between the notches) to the wrong side of the fabric. Edgestitch the turning in place.

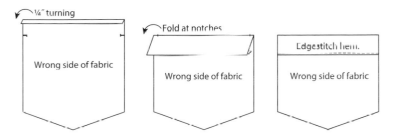

3. Press the turning on the bottom edge toward the wrong side of the fabric; then press the side turnings in the same way. Fold and press the corners of the turnings under (at an angle) so that no raw edges will accidentally poke out when the pocket is attached to the garment.

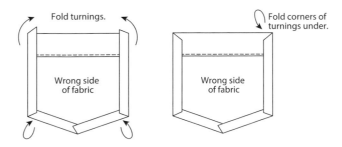

Pressing Turnings

- Use the fusible tape turning trick (page 32) to help turn straight-edge turnings.

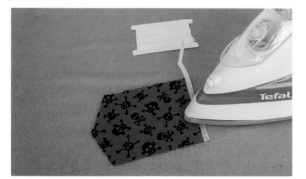

- In the absence of fusible tape, cut a cardboard template of the pocket piece without seam allowances, and use its edge to help fold the seam allowances into shape. This is particularly useful for pressing around curved or pointed pockets.

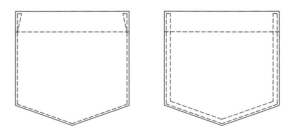

4. Place the pocket right side up on the right side of the garment, centered over the marker dots. Pin or fuse it in place. Edgestitch the pocket to the garment, reinforcing the top of each side by stitching small triangle shapes as shown. Alternatively, topstitch a second row of stitching ¼″ (6 mm) in from the first, enclosing all the raw edges of the seam allowance.

POCKET FLAPS
Skill Level: Basic

A pocket flap is completely optional on any pocket but can add interesting detail and a little extra security to a patch pocket.

Prepare the Pattern

1. Decide on the shape of the pocket flap you would like. Draw the flap in place on the draft, with the top edge ⅜" (1 cm) above the top of the pocket.

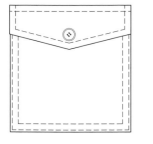

2. Trace a pattern from the draft and add a ¼" (6 mm) seam allowance around the side and lower edges and a ⅜" (1 cm) seam allowance across the top edge. Notch both side seam allowances at the top edge. Rule a grainline parallel to that on the garment and label "Cut 2" for every pocket flap that you need (so "Cut 4" for a garment with 2 pocket flaps).

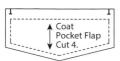

Sew the Pocket Flap

1. Cut 2 pocket flap pieces and 1 interfacing piece per pocket. Trim the seam allowances off the interfacing and fuse it, centered, to the wrong side of one of the flap pieces. The interfaced piece is now the outer flap piece.

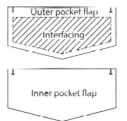

2. With the right sides of the fabric together and all edges aligned, stitch around the side and bottom edges with a ¼" seam allowance, pivoting at the corner points and backstitching at both ends of the seam.

3. Clip the corners to reduce bulk, and press the seam allowances open. If the shape of the pocket flap is curved, use pinking shears to trim the seam allowances.

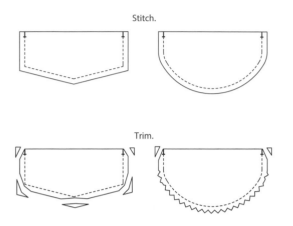

Stitch.

Trim.

4. Turn the pocket flap through to the right side, press it flat, and topstitch around the seamed edges. If you want a buttonhole or snap on the flap, attach that now.

5. Place the pocket flap above the pocket with the right sides of the flap and garment together, aligning the raw edge of the flap with the top edge of the pocket. The pocket flap will be upside down. Pin it in place, and stitch ⅜″ (1 cm) from the raw edge of the fabric, backstitching at both ends.

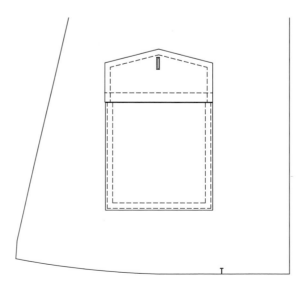

6. Trim the seam allowance to ⅛″ (3 mm), and then fold the flap over the top edge of the pocket. Press it in place from the wrong side of the garment.

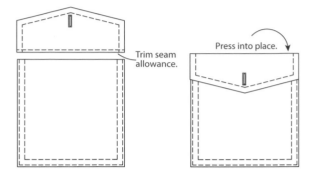

Trim seam allowance.

Press into place.

7. Topstitch ¼″ (6 mm) from the seam edge to hold the pocket flap to the fabric of the garment, trapping the raw seam allowances in between.

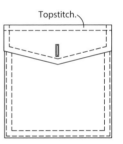

Topstitch.

Tip *Use a tailor's awl to fold and hold the seam allowances out of sight as you sew near the sides of the pocket flap.*

8. Check the placement of the pocket button or snap, and attach it to the pocket.

HIP POCKETS
Skill Level: Basic

This pocket is an easy alteration to make. It's frequently used on casual pants, jeans, skirts, and dresses.

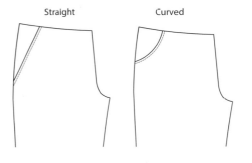

Straight   Curved

NOTE   *It is also very simple to remove the hip pockets from an existing pattern. Place the pocket back pattern on top of the garment front pattern, aligning any notches that correspond between the two pattern pieces at the top edge and side seam. Trace a new draft, following the seamlines of the hip and waist curves of the pocket back until they meet the seams of the garment front. Trace the rest of the garment front seams, and you have a complete shape that you can change to include inseam or patch pockets or leave completely plain.*

Prepare the Pattern

1. On the draft of the garment front, draw in the shape of the top edge of the pocket. Place a hand (the right size for the garment size) on the draft, as if it were sitting in the pocket, and check that there is at least ¾" (2 cm) of visible line on either side.

2. Keeping the hand on the draft, draw a rough shape for the pocket bag, ensuring that it is deep and wide enough to function comfortably as a pocket. Remove the hand and neaten the lines, squaring up from the widest part of the pocket bag to the waistline and using a curved ruler to smooth out the curved lines.

PATTERNS   FIT TOGETHER   NEW DRAFT

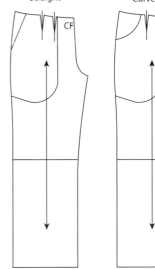
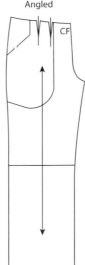

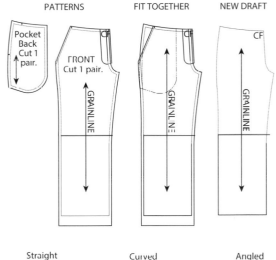

Straight   Curved   Angled

3. To allow for a pocket to drop slightly outward and not sit flat against the body, extend the side seam end of the pocket line ⅜"–½" (10–12 mm) outside the bounds of the side seam. Rule a line to blend the side seam to the end of the pocket line.

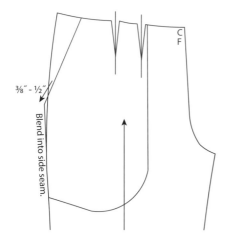

4. Trace a pattern for the front of the garment, following the new pocket line (with the side extension, if any) instead of the original hip shape. Trace all other lines, grainlines, and notches the same as on the original. Add a ¼" (6 mm) seam allowance to the pocket edge, ½" (12 mm) seam allowances to the rest of the seamlines, and your preferred hem depth at the bottom edge of the garment.

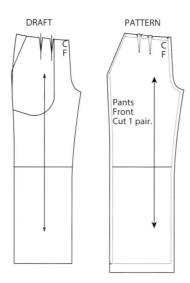

5. Trace a pattern for the pocket front, following the extended side seamline and the pocket bag line. Trace a pattern for the pocket back, following the original line of the waist and side seams and the pocket bag line. Add seam allowances all the way around (corresponding to those on the garment front pattern) and rule grainlines parallel to the grainline on the garment front. On the pocket back, notch the points where the pocket front crosses the waist and side seams.

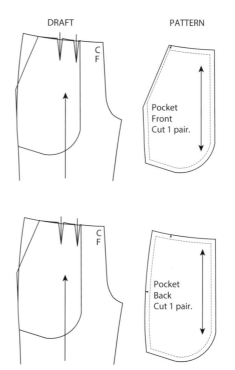

On children's wear, sleepwear, and light casual garments, you can use the main fabric for the entire pocket back.

On most adult-sized jeans or casual trousers, particularly if the fabric is heavyweight, the pocket is made of lining, with a facing (in the main fabric) that extends below the visual line of the pocket front. This means that you will cut a pocket back pattern (as in Step 5) as well as a facing pattern.

To make a facing, draw in the facing line 2″–3″ (5–7.5 cm) below the pocket shape line, curving it downward toward the center of the pocket bag. Trace a pattern from the waist and side seam to the facing line, with the grainline and all notches and seam allowances the same as on the pocket back.

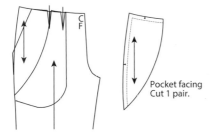

Pocket facing
Cut 1 pair.

NOTE   *When the garment is being worn, the pocket can drop down or forward with some fabrics and some garment or pocket shapes. Make a sample garment to check that the facing is wide enough and that the pocket lining doesn't show below the facing.*

You can make a facing for the edge of the pocket front, but it is often not needed. The front facing only needs to be about 1″ (2–3 cm) wide and is constructed in the same way as the facing for the pocket back.

Sew the Pocket

Instructions are written for a single pocket, but complete each step for both pockets before moving on to the next step.

1. Cut the garment pieces and the pocket back/facing from the main fabric. Cut the pocket front (and pocket back, if using a facing on it) from lining fabric. Staystitch (or sew stay tape) on the pocket line edge, if necessary.

2. If you are using a facing on the pocket back, serge around the curved bottom edge. Place the facing right side up on the pocket back, using pins or your favorite fabric adhesive to hold it in place. Topstitch along the inside edge of the serger stitch through both layers of fabric.

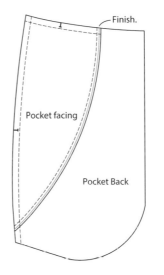

Finish.

Pocket facing

Pocket Back

3. With right sides together, match the pocket front to the garment front, and stitch the pocket line edge with a ¼″ (6 mm) seam allowance.

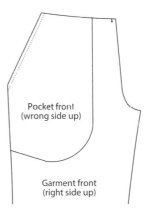

Pocket front
(wrong side up)

Garment front
(right side up)

4. Lift the pocket front to show the right side of the seam, and fold the seam allowances toward the pocket side. Understitch (page 30) along the pocket-edge seam.

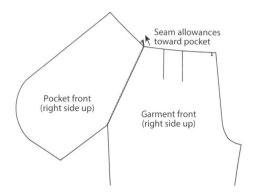

Seam allowances toward pocket

Pocket front (right side up)

Garment front (right side up)

NOTE   *If the pocket is a curved shape, take your time with understitching. Use at least three fingers on each hand to help smooth and open the seam directly in front of the needle and your thumbs underneath to keep the seam allowance flat on the back of the pocket piece.*

5. Fold the pocket front over to the wrong side of the garment (wrong sides of fabric together), and press the pocket edge. If the pocket shape is sharply curved, you may need to trim or pink the seam allowance to ⅛″ (3 mm) so that it sits flat when it's turned right side out. Topstitch ¼″ (6 mm) from the edge.

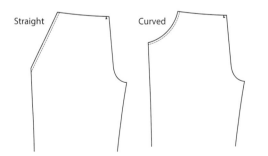

Straight   Curved

Tip   *On a straight, slanted pocket shape, fuse a strip of fusible tape to the seam allowances so that the outer garment fabric sticks to the seam allowance when you press the pocket front to the inside. This will keep the fabric from twisting or moving as you topstitch and create a sharp finish on the pocket edge.*

6. With the right sides facing up, match the garment front with the pocket back piece, aligning the waist and side seam ends of the pocket line with the notches on the pocket back. This will show you where the pocket bag pieces will be sewn together and how the whole thing comes together on the garment.

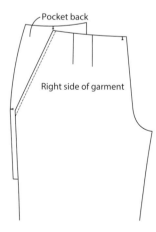

Pocket back

Right side of garment

7. Sew and finish the raw edges of the pocket bag seam. Depending on the production quality you require, you can do this in a number of ways.

PLAIN SEAMED POCKET

Hold or pin the pocket back to the pocket front, right sides together, and sew around the pocket bag edges (not catching the garment in the seam). Serge or bind the raw edges of the pocket-bag seam allowances.

FRENCH SEAMED POCKET

1. With wrong sides together, align the pocket front and back and stitch them together with a scant ¼" (4–5 mm) seam allowance.

2. Understitch the seam allowances to the pocket-front side of the seam, or press the seam allowances open. Turn the pocket through so the wrong side of the fabric is facing out. Press the seams flat, and then stitch a generous ¼" (6 mm) from the edge to enclose the seam allowances. Press the seams flat again.

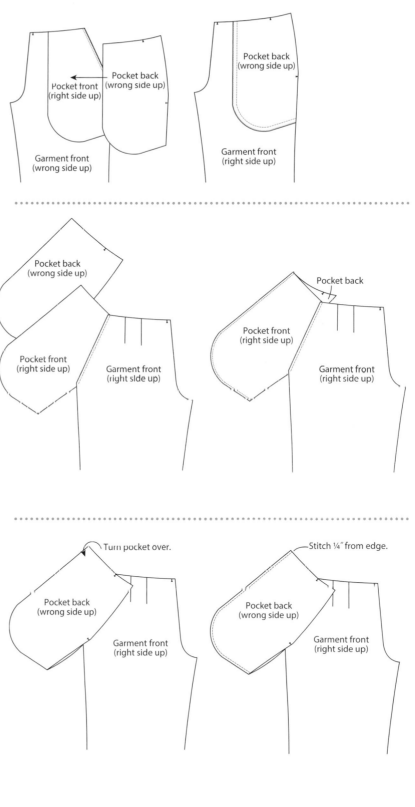

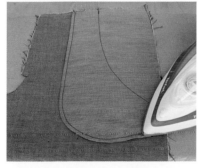

3. Align the notches on the pocket back with the pocket end on the garment, and stitch the pocket bag to the garment within the waistline and side seam allowances. You can now join the garment front and back.

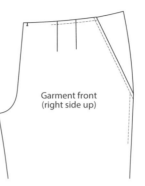

Garment front
(right side up)

INSEAM SIDE POCKETS

This pocket sits discreetly within a side seam and can easily be added to a skirt, dress, or pair of pants. There are many ways to construct an inseam pocket—these are just two of them.

Inseam pockets can be added to skirts, pants, or dresses.

Prepare the Draft

1. Trace a draft copy of the front and back garment pieces. Estimate the size of the pocket opening and mark the position of its top and bottom ends on the side seam of both drafts.

Tip *Put your hand on your hip, in an imaginary pocket, to visualize where it might be on the garment. Take the measurements from the waist.*

2. Draw the pocket shape (trace around your hand to make sure it's big enough and at the right angle) on at least one garment draft. In dresses or other loose-fitting garments, you can make the pocket completely free within the garment, joined only at the side seam.

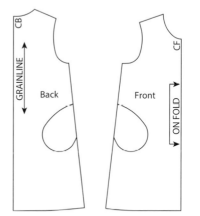

On pants, skirts, and dresses with a waist seam, the pocket bag can be shaped to join into both

the waist and side seams to take wear-and-tear pressure off the side seam opening and help the pocket to lie flat. Draw a straight line across the top of the pocket, between the waistline edge of the side seam and the inside edge of the pocket bag, and extend the side seam edge of the pocket bag at least 1″ (2.5 cm) below the bottom of the pocket opening.

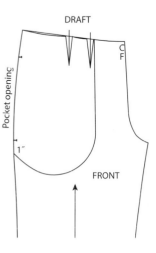

Fast-Fashion Method *Skill Level: Basic*

This is the no-fuss way to insert an inseam pocket in a relatively straight seam, and it is a good place for beginners to start. The downside of this method is that the lining of the pocket is likely to show when the garment is being worn, but it's fine if the garment fabric is light enough to use for the pocket.

Skip to Facing Method for Inseam Pocket (page 52) if you prefer a finer finish for pants and skirts.

1. Trace the garment pattern as usual, with a ½″ or ⅝″ (12 mm or 15 mm) seam allowance along the side seam. Square across from the top and bottom of the pocket opening to notch the pocket position on the seam allowance. Place dot markings at the intersections of the side seam and the pocket lines.

2. Trace the pocket pattern, with the grainline parallel to the grainline on the garment. Add a ¼″ (6 mm) seam allowance to the side seam on the pocket, and notch the top and bottom of the pocket opening to match to the side seam position marks.

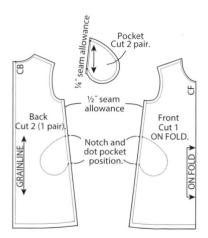

Sew the Inseam Pocket

1. Cut all the garment pieces from your chosen fabric. Cut the pocket pieces from lining or lightweight self-fabric—you will need 1 mirror pair (2 pieces) per pocket. Transfer all the notches and dot markings to the cut pieces (see Dot Markings, page 18).

2. Sew any darts, pleats, patch pockets, or other details in place on the garment pieces.

3. Serge around the curved edges of each pocket piece (do not serge the waist or side seam edges).

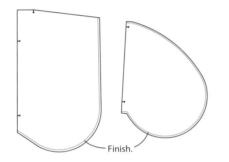

Finish.

4. With right sides together, match the pocket pieces to the front and back garment pieces, aligning the notches on the side seams. Stitch the pockets in place with a ¼″ (6 mm) seam allowance and serge/finish the full length of each side seam edge.

Tip *To save time moving between the serger and the sewing machine, I usually serge the pocket bags in place on the garment pieces as soon as I finish the edges of the pocket bags and then seam them. Try it this way only if you are confident with a serger.*

5. Turn all the pocket pieces to show the right side of the fabric. Edgestitch (page 30) a generous ¹⁄₁₆″ (2 mm) from the seam, holding the seam allowances underneath to the pocket bag side of the seam.

6. With right sides together, match the garment back to the front along the side seam edges. Align and pin through the dot markings for the pocket openings. Sew the side seams, leaving gaps for the pocket openings and backstitching at each of the dot markings.

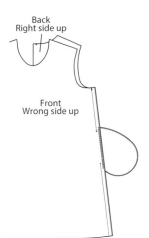

 To clearly define the pocket openings, press the pocket pieces open, creasing the garment fabric level with the side seam. You will see that the pockets start a little in from the fold.

7. Realign the pocket edges and stitch around the pockets, finishing with a backstitch at each end of the seam.

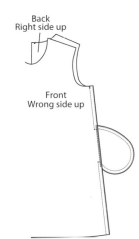

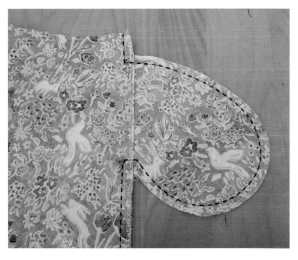

0. Turn the pockets toward the front of the garment. To enable the seam to press open all the way to the pocket, you can clip the bottom corner of the back seam allowance on a diagonal line toward the bottom of the pocket opening. (Personally, this always makes me nervous on unlined garments, and I usually just let the seam fold over at the top or serge the seam closed 1″–2″ (2.5–5 cm) below the pocket.)

9. You can bar tack (page 31) a small, tight row of zigzag stitches at both ends of each pocket opening, holding the pocket in place behind the garment front.

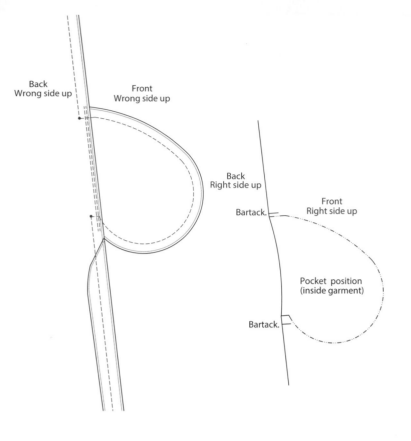

Facing Method for Inseam Pocket *Skill Level: Basic to Intermediate*

This method allows you to make an inseam pocket on a fitted garment (with a hip curve on the side seam) with a facing that hides the lining from view. The pocket front and back patterns are slightly different, and the bottom of the pocket extends into the side seam, so the construction is slightly different. There are many ways to make this pocket, and I've chosen to share one that is suitable for unlined skirts, pants, and dresses for everyday wear.

NOTE *For light, summer-weight fabric, you can make this pocket in the same fabric as the garment, which eliminates the need for a facing. Cut and sew the pocket back as one piece.*

PREPARE THE PATTERN

1. On the draft of the garment front, draw the pocket shape extended to the waist and side seam, as shown in Inseam Side Pockets, Prepare the Draft (page 48). Trace the placement notches through to the back draft, in exactly the same position on the side seam.

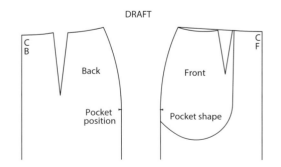

2. On the pocket shape, draw in the shape of the facing, allowing at least 2″ (5 cm) width (more for larger pockets) at the center of the pocket opening. The facing line can be straight or curved. It's easier to sew if it's straight, but it allows for more width at the center without extra bulk if it's curved. On both the pocket and facing, draw in the grainline parallel to the grainline on the garment front.

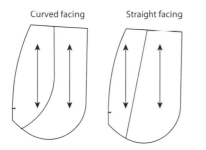

Curved facing   Straight facing

3. Trace the garment patterns, adding seam allowances all the way around. Notch the pocket placements on the side seams of both front and back pieces. Trace the patterns for the pocket pieces—a full pocket shape for the pocket front, a facing, and the pocket back (which is traced only to the facing line). Add seam allowances all the way around all the pieces.

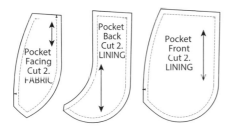

Pocket Facing Cut 2. FABRIC

Pocket Back Cut 2. LINING

Pocket Front Cut 2. LINING

NOTE   *Alternatively, make the pocket lining front and back from the same pattern, and cut a separate facing pattern. When you sew the pocket, the facing will be overlaid and stitched onto the back lining instead of setting the two pieces together (see Hip Pockets, Sew the Pocket, page 45).*

4. Make a test garment using the new patterns. Check the depth and shape of the pocket and facing, and tweak the pattern if necessary.

SEW THE POCKET

1. For each pocket on the garment, cut 1 pocket front from the lining, 1 pocket back from the lining, and 1 pocket facing from the garment fabric.

NOTE   *If you are making the pocket with an overlaid facing, follow the instructions in Hip Pockets, Sew the Pocket (page 45) to attach the facing to the pocket back piece.*

2. With right sides together, sew the facing to the pocket back, backstitching at each end. Serge the seam allowances closed and press them in whichever way they sit flattest. You may choose to edgestitch the facing or lining to hold the seam allowances in place.

SETTING IN A CURVED FACING WITHOUT PINS

It's faster and often easier to set convex and con-cave pieces together without pins, because the fabric is easier to manipulate smoothly and you won't scratch yourself on the sharp ends. Work with the facing (convex curve) on top as the seam goes into the machine. With your right hand, hold the two pieces together at the end of the curve. Use three fingers on your left hand to hold the facing along the seamline as you align the outer edges of the seam allowances. Repositioning your fingers to maintain the alignment as the fabric moves through the machine, stitch with an accu-rate seam allowance.

3. With right sides together, place the pocket front (without the facing) on the garment front, aligning the side seams and notches. With a ½˝ (12 mm) seam allowance and backstitching at both ends of the seam, stitch from the top of the side seam to level with the notch (that marks the bottom of the pocket) on the side seam.

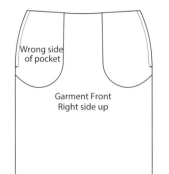

Wrong side of pocket

Garment Front
Right side up

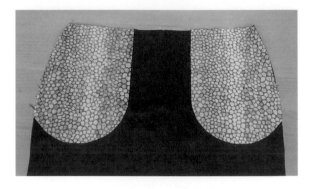

4. Turn the pocket front to show the right side of the seam and understitch (page 30) on the pocket lining, stopping level with the notch.

5. Snip into the seam allowance ¼˝ (6 mm) above the notch to a scant ⅛˝ (2.5 mm) from the understitched seam. (Don't cut too close to the stitches.) Trim or pink the seam allow-ances above this snip to ⅛˝ (3 mm).

Tip *To make a crisp topstitched edge on the pocket opening (Step 7, next page), fuse a strip of ¼˝ (6 mm) fusible tape alongside the pocket seam on the wrong side of the outer fabric now.*

Pocket front

Fusible tape

Garment Front
Wrong side of fabric

6. Press the pocket front to the inside of the garment. As you match the pocket and garment side seams, turn the raw edges of the seam allowances below the notch inward (at about a 45° angle) and out of sight. Use a fabric glue stick to hold the folded edges together and enclose the raw edges.

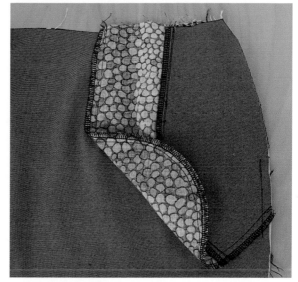

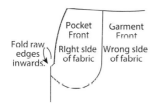

Fold raw edges inwards.

Pocket Front	Garment Front
Right side of fabric	Wrong side of fabric

7. Topstitch ¼" (6 mm) from the edge along the full length of the pocket. Pivot at notch level and stitch toward the raw edge of the fabric.

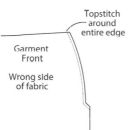

Topstitch around entire edge

Garment Front

Wrong side of fabric

8. Match the pocket front to back, right sides together; then seam and serge (or bind) the curved edges. Stitch the side seam edges of the pocket in place on the garment front, ⅜" (1 cm) from the edge.

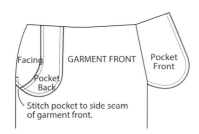

Facing   GARMENT FRONT   Pocket Front

Pocket Back

Stitch pocket to side seam of garment front.

9. With right sides together, align the **side seam edges** of the garment front and back. Stitch the side seam from the waist to the hemline, keeping the front edge of the pocket out of the seam. Serge the side seam allowances.

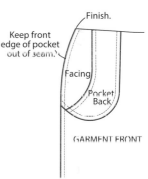

Finish.

Keep front edge of pocket out of seam.

Facing

Pocket Back

GARMENT FRONT

10. Press the side seam allowances toward the back of the garment. For (optional) reinforcement at the top and bottom of the pocket opening, make a ⅜" (1 cm) bar tack (page 31) to hold the pocket and side seams toward the garment back.

11. Stitch the garment and pocket together at the top edge (within the seam allowance) to hold them in place before attaching a waistband or bodice.

Button Plackets and Facings

A button placket is the straight bound (usually CF) edge on the garment that holds the buttons and buttonholes. It is often made from a separate piece of fabric that is topstitched in place. A button facing serves the same purpose but is generally not topstitched around all the edges; its inner edge sits loose on the inside of the garment. A button facing can be a straight piece on the button extension edge or include the shape of the neckline.

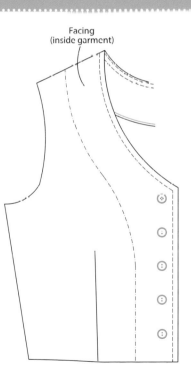

Facing
(inside garment)

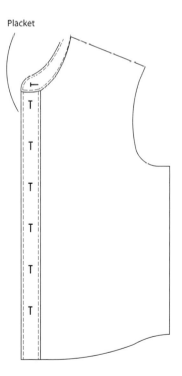

Placket

These are a few of the methods for adding button plackets and facings on shirts, dresses, and tops with collars, and they can be interchanged endlessly. They all begin with drafting the button extension (or button stand), which extends a little beyond the center of the garment and holds the buttons and buttonholes.

ADDING THE BUTTON EXTENSION

NOTE

This is the beginning point for constructing all the button plackets and facings. Complete these steps before following the individual instructions for the various styles.

1. To change a button extension or add one to any pattern, first find the CF on your pattern and decide what size button you'd like to use. Trace a draft of the shirt front with a noticeable vertical line marking the CF.

2. Measure outward from the CF the distance of the button diameter that you are using (for example, a ½″ [12 mm] button = ½″ [12 mm] button extension), and draw a line at this distance, parallel to the CF. Square across at the top and bottom to join the extension to the shirt front.

3. On the garment side of the CF, draw another parallel line at the same distance from the CF as the extension. This is the placket/facing line, which marks the shape of the placket or facing.

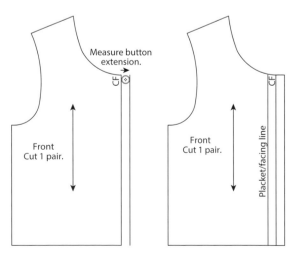

You can now move on to make the pattern for the button placket or facing of your choice.

FOLDED FACING
Skill Level: Basic

This is a "grown on" extension to the button stand, which folds back to form a clean-edged finish. It's a simple way to make a button facing on blouses, dresses, and shirts where no stitched detail is desired in the design. It can be used with a Peter Pan collar (page 145) as well as with a classic collar and stand (page 125).

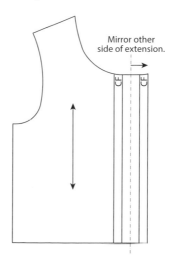

Prepare the Pattern

1. Make a draft copy of the garment and add a button extension (previous page). Trace a pattern from the draft, including the button extension.

2. Flip the pattern paper over to trace a mirror image of the facing from the draft on the other side of the extension. (You should be able to see the lines through the paper on the right side of the pattern.)

3. Add a ¼" (6 mm) seam allowance to the outer edge of the facing and your preferred seam allowances around all the other edges. Notch all 4 CF positions on the neckline and hemline seam allowances.

4. Trace a pattern for the interfacing using the facing shape of the pattern, including the seam allowances.

Mirror other side of extension.

CF   CF

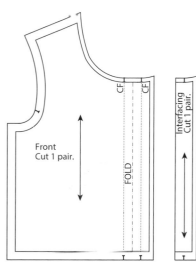

Front
Cut 1 pair.

CF   CF

FOLD

Interfacing
Cut 1 pair.

Sew the Folded Facing

1. Cut 1 pair of facing pieces from lightweight interfacing for the facings and fuse to the wrong side of the fabric on both facing edges.

2. Serge the inside edges of the facings, and/or press a ¼″ (6 mm) turning toward the wrong side, and edgestitch a generous ¹⁄₁₆″ (exactly 2 mm) from the fold.

3. Fold and press the facing toward the wrong side of the fabric, matching the CF notches of the facing to the garment at both the neckline and hemline edges. You may now construct the garment and attach the collar.

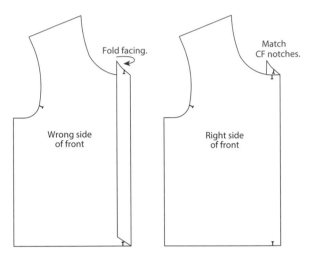

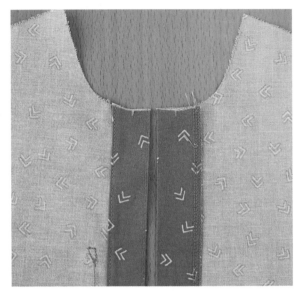

Two different edge finishes: turned edge or serging

SEPARATE PLACKET OR FACING

Skill Level: Basic to Intermediate

This is an easy way to construct a placket for a classic shirt, and it can *only* be used with a classic collar and stand or mandarin collar (which is a collar stand without the collar). You will need to draft a new collar (see Classic Shirt Collar and Stand, page 125) if the pattern you are using has any other collar style.

The separate placket is topstitched to the right side of the fabric, giving definition and structure to the overwrap of the garment. The facing is on the inside of the underwrap—it can be topstitched or simply held in place by the buttons.

Prepare the Pattern

1. Make a draft copy (page 21) of the garment front with a button extension (page 58). Trace a pattern from the draft, including the button extension. Add a ¼″ (6 mm) seam allowance to the button extension edge and your preferred seam allowances to the other edges.

2. Trace a pattern for the placket/facing, from the button extension line to the placket/facing line and from the neckline to the hemline. Add a ¼″ (6 mm) seam allowance at each vertical edge and seam allowances to match the garment at the neckline and hemline.

3. Make a pattern without seam allowances for the interfacing for the placket/facing.

DRAFT

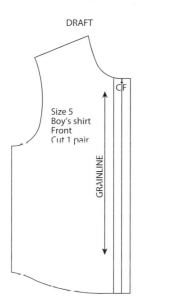

Size 5
Boy's shirt
Front
Cut 1 pair

CF

GRAINLINE

PATTERNS

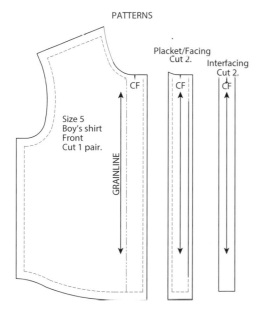

Size 5
Boy's shirt
Front
Cut 1 pair.

GRAINLINE

CF

Placket/Facing
Cut 2.

CF

Interfacing
Cut 2.

CF

Sew the Placket and Facing

1. Cut 1 mirror pair of shirt fronts. Cut 2 (not a mirror pair) each of the placket/facing and interfacing, so that the right side of fabric will face upwards on the buttonhole side. Fuse the interfacing to the wrong side of the placket and facing pieces (between the seam allowances).

2. Along the inside edge of the placket, press a ¼″ (6 mm) turning toward the interfacing. (You can use the fusible tape turning trick, page 32.)

3. On the buttonhole side, place the right side of the placket to the wrong side of the shirt, aligning the CF notches and front seam edges. Stitch the front edge seam with a ¼″ (6 mm) seam allowance.

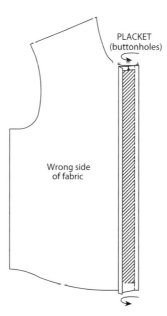

PLACKET
(buttonholes)

Wrong side
of fabric

4. Clip the corners and press the seam allowance open or to one side of the seam.

5. Turn the placket over to the right side of the shirt front, pressing to crease along the seam.

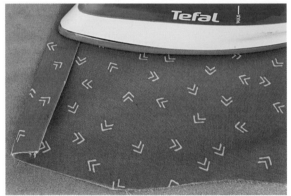

6. Pin or fuse the turned edge of the placket to the right side of the fabric, and edgestitch both sides of the placket a scant ⅛″ (2–3 mm) from the edges.

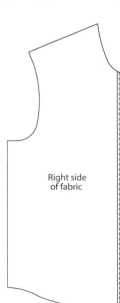

Right side of fabric

7. Align the facing and other shirt front with right sides together, and stitch the front edge seam. Press and edgestitch the facing onto the wrong side of the fabric in the same manner as the buttonhole placket (Step 6, below left).

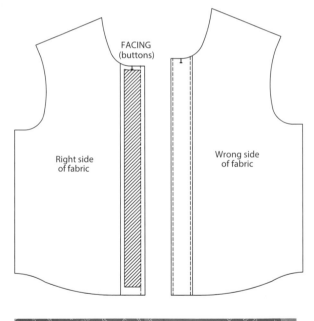

FACING (buttons)

Right side of fabric

Wrong side of fabric

Facing on the inside of the garment and button placket on the right side of the fabric

CLASSIC SHIRT PLACKET

Skill Level: Intermediate

This is a folded placket and facing that gives the defined, structured effect of a sewn-on placket with a topstitched tuck that encloses the raw edges of the facing. Although it may look a little complicated at first, it's a very quick, neat way to make a professional-looking classic shirt.

This placket can only be used with a classic collar and stand or mandarin collar (which is a collar stand without the collar). You will need to draft a collar (see Classic Shirt Collar and Stand, page 125) if the pattern you are using has any other sort of collar.

Prepare the Pattern

1. Make a draft copy of the garment front with a button extension (page 58). Trace a pattern for the shirt front from the side seam to the placket/facing line only, as shown (not the CF or button extension line).

2. On the pattern paper, rule a parallel line ½" (12 mm) out from the placket/facing line. Square out to extend the hemline about 3" (7.5 cm) over the CF area. This area will be the tuck in the placket.

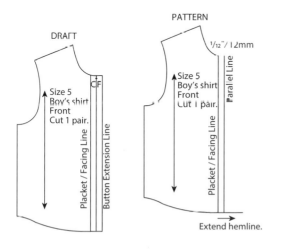

3. Align the parallel line on the pattern with the placket/facing line on the draft and match the extended hemline on the pattern to the hemline on the draft. Trace the placket shape onto the pattern, leaving a ½" (12 mm) gap between the shirt and placket (for the tuck). Mark the CF on the neckline edge.

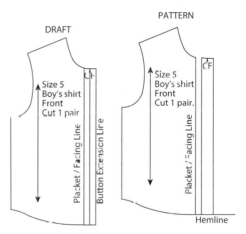

4. Fold the pattern along the outer line of the button extension, and trace a "grown on" facing for the placket, mirroring the shape of the placket.

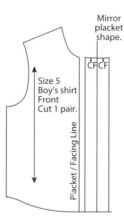

5. Add a ¼″ (6 mm) seam allowance to the edge of the facing and the neckline (except on the tuck). Add your preferred seam allowance to all the other edges of the pattern. Notch the top and bottom of the fold line between the mirrored placket and facing. Extend both ends of the parallel lines that form the tuck through the seam allowances. Draw a vertical line through the very center of the tuck.

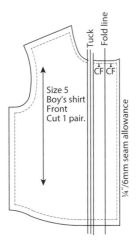

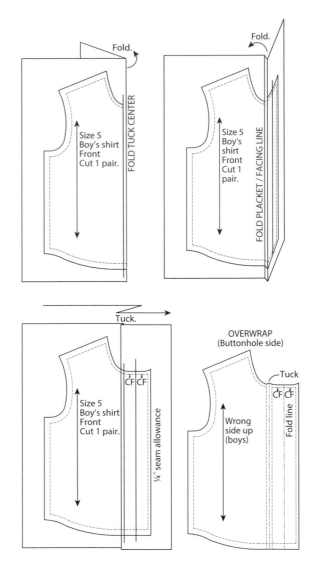

6. Fold and crease the pattern along the line through the center of the tuck so that the parallel lines on either side of the tuck meet. Fold and crease the original placket/facing line so the tuck sits in place over the shirt body. With the tuck folded in this position, cut along the neckline seam allowance so the seam allowances of the tuck are shaped to fit to the neckline.

7. The tuck detail is only on the overwrap (buttonhole side) of the shirt. The underwrap (button side) can be a folded facing made with the same pattern piece, but the notches need to be different. I'd recommend marking the underwrap notches on the other side of the pattern paper from the overwrap or cutting a separate pattern piece for this side.

8. To finish the pattern for the underwrap, rule parallel lines to move both the facing fold line and the outer seamline of the facing ½″ (12 mm) closer to the shirt body. Notch the top and bottom of these lines on the seam allowances.

(*Tip:* If making a separate pattern piece for each side, you can fold the underwrap pattern along the new lines and "true" the neckline by cutting along the neckline seam allowance edge in a smooth curve.) Mark "Right side up" or "Wrong side up" on the pattern to indicate how to match it to the fabric.

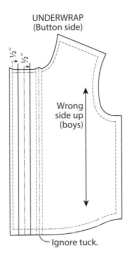

UNDERWRAP
(Button side)

Wrong side up (boys)

Ignore tuck.

9. For the placket interfacing, trace the facing section of the garment pattern from the fold line to the outer edge. Mark it "Cut 1."

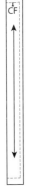

INTERFACING
(Right side up)

CF

Sew the Placket and Facing

1. Cut the shirt fronts, and carefully mark the appropriate notches for the classic placket and folded facing. Cut interfacing for the buttonhole placket, and fuse it to the wrong side of the fabric on the overwrap side of the garment.

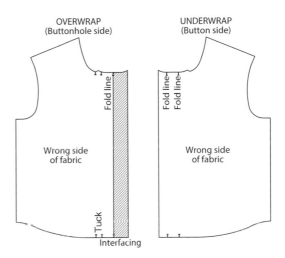

OVERWRAP
(Buttonhole side)

UNDERWRAP
(Button side)

Fold line

Fold line

Fold line

Wrong side of fabric

Wrong side of fabric

Tuck

Interfacing

2. On the underwrap side of the garment, fold the facing between the first set of notches (¾" [2 cm] in from the raw edge) toward the wrong side of the fabric, and press a crease. Fold between the next set of notches to turn the facing onto the wrong side of the fabric and press it in place. That's all; the buttons will anchor the facing to the garment.

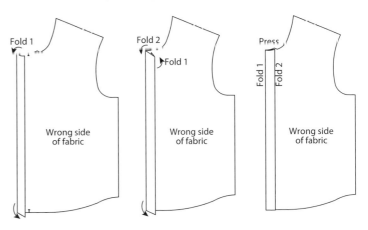

Fold 1

Fold 2

Fold 1

Press

Fold 1

Fold 2

Wrong side of fabric

Wrong side of fabric

Wrong side of fabric

5. Lift the placket from the wrong side of the fabric, and topstitch the outside edge ¼″ (6 mm) from the fold.

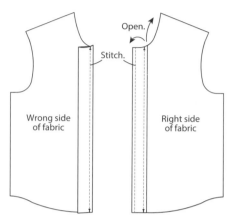

3. On the buttonhole side of the garment, fold at the first set of notches to press the facing to the wrong side of the fabric. Fold along the center of the tuck, matching the notches on either side, and press a sharp crease. The raw edge of the facing seam allowance should sit inside the tuck.

6. Press the placket flat, with the tuck facing toward the body of the shirt. Continue to construct the garment.

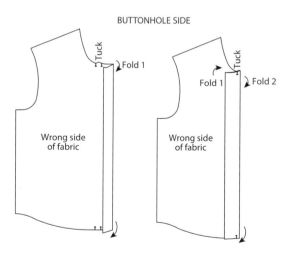

4. Keeping the fabric pressed in place, topstitch ¼″ (6 mm) from the folded edge of the tuck.

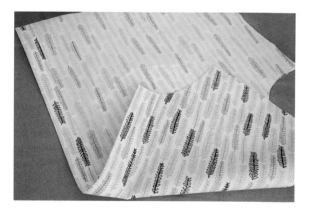

HEMLINES, PLACKETS, AND FACINGS

Skill Level: Basic

Where a topstitched placket meets a hemline, it will be turned and stitched with the rest of the garment hemline as if part of the same fabric. On a blouse, shirt, or dress, "bagging out" the facing at the hemline can be a neat finish.

1. Fold the facing toward the right side of the garment, aligning the hemline edge. Stitch across the bottom of the facing at the hem depth, backstitching at each end.

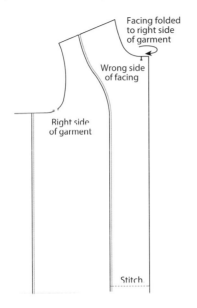

Facing folded to right side of garment

Wrong side of facing

Right side of garment

Stitch

2. Turn the facings to the right side, and press them and the hem in place on the wrong side of the fabric. For dresses and skirts, serge and blind hem (see Blind Hem Foot, page 13).

For shirts and blouses, make a double-turned hem—fold and press the raw edges in toward the crease line and edgestitch along the fold of the turning.

 For curved hemlines, use the stitched guide turning trick (page 31).

NOTE

You can begin the hemming stitch on the inner edge of the facing, just catching it with a few stitches to hold it in place, or you can stitch the hem depth through the full width of the facing.

MARKING AND SEWING BUTTONS

Skill Level: Basic

Buttons and buttonholes are sewn along the CF of a shirt or dress. You can decide on their placement once the garment is finished. Buttonholes are placed vertically on shirts (but a collar stand always has a horizontal buttonhole) and horizontally on waistcoats, jackets, and coats. For dresses and blouses with wide buttonhole facings, the buttonholes can be placed horizontally (to allow for more movement) or vertically (for more stability). The "rules" keep changing here, so do what works for you.

1. Use the pattern to establish the distance of the CF from the edge of the button extension on your finished garment.

2. Arrange the buttons on top of the overwrap side of the garment, spacing them in an arrangement that pleases you, which will depend on the sizes of both the buttons and the garment. Make sure that there are buttons level with the bust and waist so that the garment will not gape when it's worn. Using a tape measure or ruler, make sure the buttons are evenly spaced.

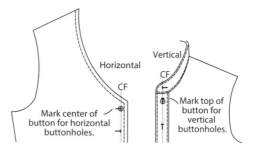

3. At the CF on the overwrap (or placket), mark the position of the top buttonhole. For vertical buttonholes, mark level with the top of the top button. For horizontal buttonholes, mark level with the center of the top button.

4. Measure the distance between these marks and mark the CF at this distance for each buttonhole that you need. On horizontal buttonholes, mark each buttonhole a scant ⅛" (2 mm) to the button extension side of the CF so the opening of the buttonhole will begin right on the CF.

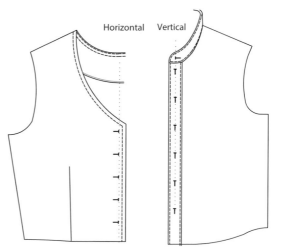

5. Follow the instructions in your sewing machine manual to make the buttonholes ⅛"–¼" (3–6 mm) longer than the diameter of the buttons. The buttonhole length depends as much on the thickness of the button as it does the diameter, so make a test buttonhole or two in a scrap of your garment fabric before you stitch the buttonholes in the garment.

6. Cut the space in the middle of the button-holes with the sharpest, pointiest scissors you own without cutting through any stitches.

7. Place the garment right side up on your work surface, with the buttonholes over the CF of the underwrap side of the garment. Align the neckline and hemlines, and stick a pin through each buttonhole—at the CF end of a horizontal buttonhole and through the middle of a vertical buttonhole. Lift the buttonhole side away and move the pins to the true CF, or mark the CF position with a fabric marker.

8. Sew a button at each pin position.

Tip *When sewing flat buttons, place a tailor's awl or tapestry needle between the button and fabric as you sew. Before you tie off the thread, remove the awl and wrap the needle and thread several times around the button. This creates a "shank" with the loose threads underneath the button, allowing space for the buttonholes to sit around and under the button.*

Necklines

NECKLINE FACINGS

A facing is placed on the inside of a garment opening (such as a neckline, waist, armhole, or pocket top) and is usually made of the same fabric as the outer garment. It completely encloses the raw edges of the fabric and maintains visual continuity between the outer garment and what can be seen of the inside. With interfacing attached to its underside, a facing also acts as a structural support, defining the edge of a garment.

A facing is an easy addition to a garment pattern since it mostly follows the existing lines of the outer garment shape. So If you're new to pattern adjustments, changing a neckline shape is a good place to start. You can then move on to adding or removing collars.

NOTE

Drastically lowering the neckline of a garment that fits loosely around the shoulders and upper chest can be tricky, as the neckline may gape. It's best to start with styles that fit closely to the upper chest area.

The neckline shape can be changed.

A collar can be added or removed.

FACINGS FOR BACK ZIPPERED CLOSURES

Skill Level: Basic to Intermediate

You can make this alteration on any well-fitting top or dress to lower or change the shape of a neckline or to remove buttons and/or a collar and add a zipper at the CB.

Prepare the Pattern

1. Trace a draft of the front and back without any seam allowances or button extensions (trace only to the CF or CB). Mark the draft to cut the CF on the fold (see When to Cut on Fold, page 22).

NOTE

If you are making a dress with separate skirt pieces, make the same alterations to the CF and CB seamlines on the skirt pieces as you do on the bodice pieces. The waistline and hemline will remain as they were.

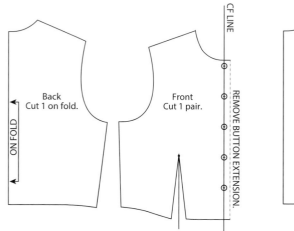

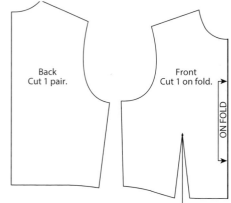

2. Draw the new neckline if you'd like to change it from the existing design. You can make it lower, higher, or a different shape (rounded, V-shaped, square).

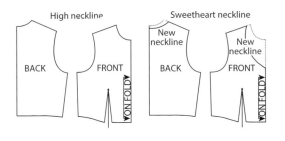

High neckline

BACK   FRONT

Sweetheart neckline

New neckline   BACK   New neckline   FRONT

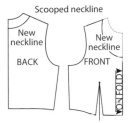

Scooped neckline

New neckline   BACK   New neckline   FRONT

NOTE

If you are working on a garment with a raglan sleeve, trace the draft with the sleeve attached to both front and back (at least at the neckline, if the pieces don't align all the way to the underarm) so that you can change the neckline as if it were one piece.

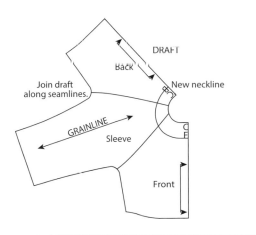

DRAFT

Back

Join draft along seamlines.   New neckline

GRAINLINE

Sleeve

Front

3. Trace patterns for the front and back, add seam allowances, and sew a quick test garment to check the pattern. Make any necessary changes to the shape of the neckline on the pattern, and test it again until you are happy with it.

4. Draw the shape of the facing on both the front and back bodice drafts (or around the whole neckline on a raglan), keeping the line relatively parallel with the neckline. The depth of the facing can be anywhere between 2″ and 4″ (5 cm and 10 cm), depending on the scale of the garment (narrower for children's wear, wider for adult sizes). Make sure that the facing pieces are the same width where they meet at the front and back shoulder.

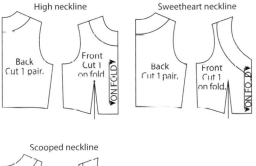

High neckline

Back Cut 1 pair.   Front Cut 1 on fold

Sweetheart neckline

Back Cut 1 pair.   Front Cut 1 on fold.

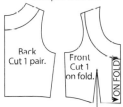

Scooped neckline

Back Cut 1 pair.   Front Cut 1 on fold.

5. Trace the garment patterns with the CF on the fold and the CB on a seam. For a lapped zipper, make the CB seam allowance ⅝″ (1.5 cm), and for an invisible zipper, make ½″ (12 mm) seam allowances. Add your preferred seam allowances on all the other edges.

If the pattern is a dress pattern with separate skirt pieces, make the CB, waist, and side seam allowances match the bodice pattern. Notch the position of the CB seam on the neckline seam allowance, and notch the length of the zipper on the CB seam allowance (this may be below the waist level on a dress, on the back skirt pattern).

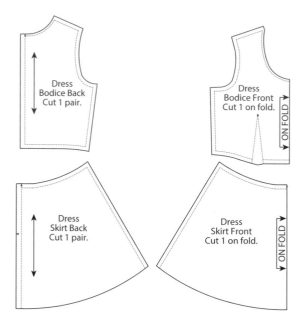

6. Trace the facing patterns, adding seam allowances on the CB, shoulder, and neckline edges to match those on the garment pieces (above). Mark the CF "Cut on fold," and draw the grainline on the back facing parallel to the CB seam. Notch the position of the CB seam on the top of the neckline seam allowance.

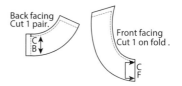

SEW THE FACING

1. Cut 1 front facing (on the fold) and 1 pair of back facings from fabric. Cut and fuse light-weight fusible interfacing to all the facing pieces. (I prefer to block fuse the interfacing, page 33, before cutting.)

2. Place the back and front facing pieces right sides together, taking care not to confuse the CB and side seams on the back facings. Sew the shoulder seams, backstitching at each end.

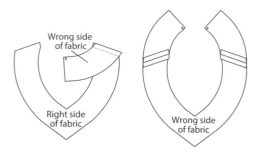

3. Either serge the seam allowances together and press them toward the front, or serge (or pink) them individually and press them open. Clip the corners at the neckline end of the shoulder seam allowances to reduce bulk.

4. Serge around the outer edge of the neck facing.

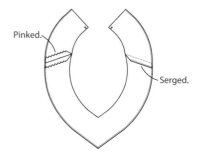

ATTACH THE FACING

The process for attaching the facing to a zippered closure varies according to the style of zipper used. See Lapped Zipper with a Facing (page 93) or Attaching a Facing to an Invisible Zipper (page 88) .

NECKLINE FACING AND BUTTON CLOSURE

Skill Level: Basic

This technique combines a basic button facing with a neckline facing. It can be used on a collarless neckline, with a Peter Pan collar (page 145), or with a convertible collar (page 136).

Once you know how to alter patterns this way, you can really make the most of your favorites. It's an especially handy trick for simple dresses and blouses for children. If you have a pattern that has a zipper or button closure on the front or back, you can interchange those features and reverse their placement. You can also lower or change the neckline shape and replace collars with scooped or sweetheart necklines.

A dress with a zippered back can be altered to make a shirt-style dress by creating a button placket through the front of the garment, with or without a collar.

Read and bookmark Adding the Button Extension (page 58) and Facings for Back Zippered Closures (page 72) before you begin.

Prepare the Pattern

In these instructions, I will make a CF button closure. The same process applies for the CB if you replace the instructions for the CF with the CB.

1. Trace a draft of the pattern pieces with the CF and CB clearly marked. Add a button extension (page 58) to the CF and draw in the new neckline shape. If you are altering a dress, also add the same button extension to the CF of the skirt piece.

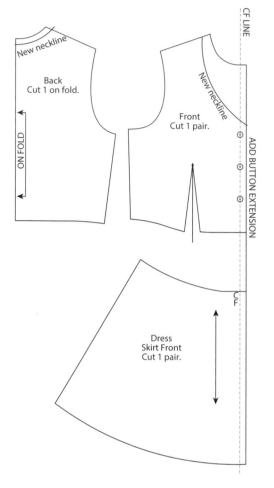

2. Trace the patterns for the front and back, add seam allowances, and sew a quick test garment to check the pattern. Make any necessary changes to the shape of the neckline on the pattern, and test it again until you are happy with it.

3. Rule a line parallel to the button extension to make a facing for the CF buttons. It can be any width between 1½″ (4 cm) and 4″ (10 cm) but should be at least 2½ times the width of the extension added at the CF. If you're making a dress, also add a facing to the front skirt piece (it can be narrower than the bodice facing).

4. Draw in the shape of the neckline facing 2″–4″ (5–10 cm) below the neckline (depending on the scale of the garment) and relatively parallel to the neckline edge, finishing where it meets the button facing. Make sure the shoulder seams of the front and back facings are the same length. Draw a curve to smooth over the join of the neckline and button facings.

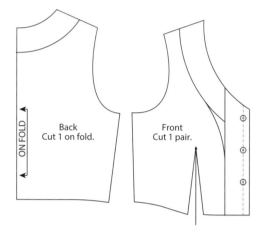

TRACE THE PATTERN

1. Trace the facing patterns, adding seam allowances to the neckline, shoulder, and CF edges. Draw the grainline parallel to the CF. Notch the CF on the neckline and waistline seam allowance. Mark the CB as "Cut on fold" (page 22).

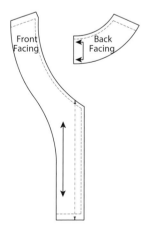

To add a convertible collar, see Convertible Collar (page 136).

2. Trace the garment patterns. Label the CB as "Cut on fold," and add seam allowances to all but the CB seam. Notch the CF on the neckline and waistline seam allowance, and place the straight grainlines parallel to the CF.

NOTE

For a dress with a separate skirt, make a folded facing on the skirt by tracing the width of the facing outside the button extension line, mirroring any waistline and hemline curves (see Folded Facing, page 59).

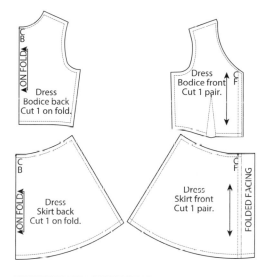

SEW AND ATTACH THE FACING

1. Match the facing fronts to the backs, right sides together. Align and sew the shoulder seams, backstitching at each end. Serge the seam allowance, and trim the neckline corners.

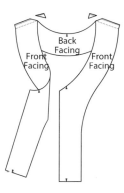

2. Press the seam allowances to the front, and serge all the way around the edges that do not attach to the garment (*not* the neckline, button extension, or hemline edges).

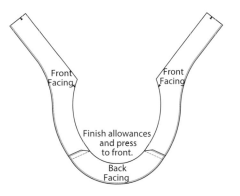

3. With right sides together, align and sew the shoulder seams of the garment, backstitching at each end. Trim the neckline corners, serge the seam allowances, and press them toward the back. Staystitch the neckline edge.

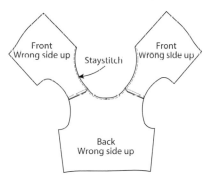

NOTE

If you are attaching a Peter Pan collar, stitch it to the neckline now (see Peter Pan Collar, page 145).

4. With right sides together, match the neckline and button edges of the facing to the garment, aligning the shoulder seams and the CF and CB notches. Stitch them together around this edge, keeping an accurate seam allowance and pivoting on the neckline corner point.

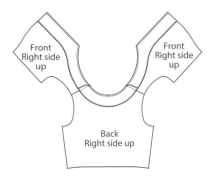

5. Understitch (page 30) the neckline of the facing a generous 1/16″ (2 mm) from the seam, catching all the seam allowances to the facing. Trim or pink the seam allowance to a generous 1/8″ (4 mm) beyond the edge stitch.

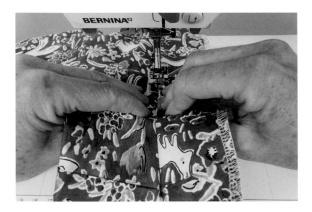

6. Press the button-edge seam allowances open; then press the whole facing flat to the inside of the garment. (Pressing the seam open will help make the seam fold sharply.)

7. If you wish, you may choose to topstitch around the entire edge of the facing.

8. Pin the shoulder seam allowance of the garment to the edge of the facing. Backstitch a discreet but secure 1/4″ (6 mm) to attach the pieces together without stitching on the outside of the garment.

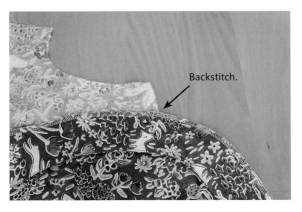

9. If you are altering a dress pattern, see Attaching a Skirt with a Folded Button Facing (page 113).

RAISING A LOW NECKLINE TO ADD A COLLAR

You can substantially raise the neckline of a garment to add a collar. A scooped neckline can be altered by either blending it with a similar-sized pattern that has a fitted neckline or by draping the neckline shape on a dress form. For both methods, the first step is to trace a draft copy of the pattern (page 21). If the bodice was previously cut with a seam (perhaps for a zipper) at the CB, mark "Cut on fold" along the CB line.

Blending Patterns · *Skill Level: Intermediate*

1. Using another pattern with a fitted neckline, match the CF and shoulder lines to those on the draft and trace the neckline through to the draft.

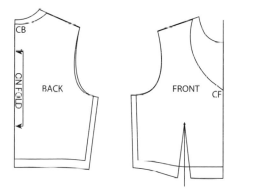

2. Add a button extension (page 58) to the CF or CB as desired if the existing pattern does not include one.

3. Trace the new patterns from the draft and add seam allowances all the way around. Make a test garment to assess and tweak the fit.

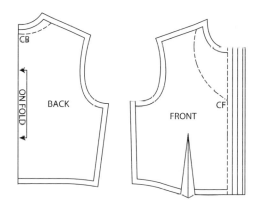

Draping a pattern involves fitting muslin around a dress form, drawing in the new garment lines, and then tracing these back onto the draft.

1. On the draft, extend the shoulder line on the front bodice toward the CF, and extend the CF line upward until it nearly meets the extended shoulder line. Do the same on the back bodice.

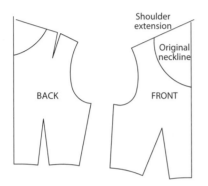

2. Trace the bodice patterns and add seam allowances all the way around, notching the point where the original neckline crossed the shoulder seam.

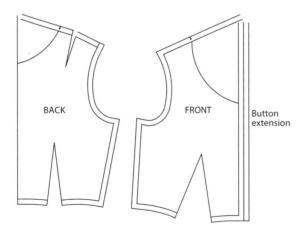

3. Cut the pattern from muslin. Sew any darts or design lines, and then sew the bodice together at the side seams. Sew the shoulder seam together between the original neckline notch and the outer edge of the shoulder.

4. Fit the muslin to a dress form, pinning it along the CF and CB to keep the grain of the fabric straight along these lines. Pin the shoulder seam together ¼" (6 mm) from the base of the neck. Trim off the excess muslin, leaving about ¾" (2 cm) above the base of the neck.

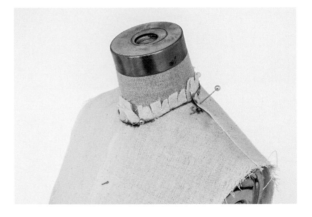

5. To allow the fabric to drape around the neckline, cut ½" (12 mm) snips every ½" (12 mm) or so into the remaining excess muslin around the neckline. Smooth the muslin from the shoulder and chest, snipping deeper into those

neckline snips if necessary, until the fabric fits around the shape of the dress form without any puckers. Adjust the shoulder seam if necessary. Draw a new neckline onto the muslin, staying close to the base of the neck.

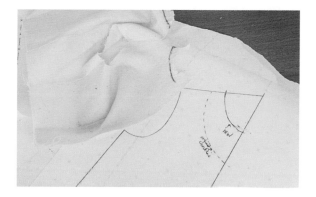

6. Trace the new neckline back onto the draft. Refer to Proving or Trueing a Line (page 25) to true (or prove) the draft by matching the front and back shoulder seams together. Use a curved ruler to redraw the neckline, making it a single smooth curved line that crosses from back to front. Square across the last $3/16''$ (5 mm) at the CF and CB. Add a button extension at the CF (page 58) or the correct seam allowance for a zippered closure (page 83), according to your desired design.

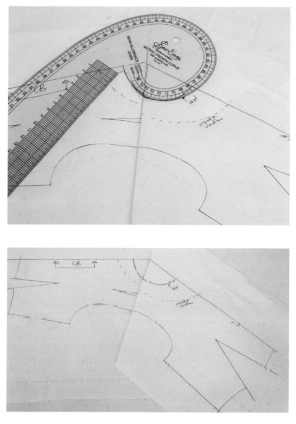

7. Trace a pattern, and then make a test garment to try on a dress form or person. If the neckline appears too tight, mark or trim the muslin where it might be more comfortable. If it is too low or wide, make a note of how much you need to add to the pattern at the various points around the neckline. Make any necessary changes to the draft copy of the bodice and adjust your pattern pieces with these alterations.

Zippered Closures

INVISIBLE ZIPPER

Skill Level: Basic to Intermediate

An invisible zipper has the chain on the underside, and the closed zipper looks almost like the continuation of a seam. Invisible zippers are used mostly on neckline and waistline openings, but once you learn how easy it is to set in this type of zipper, you'll want to use them on everything.

If you have a pattern for a garment using a lapped or centered zipper application, you can convert it by making the seam allowances ⅜″ or ½″ (10 mm or 12 mm) and then following these instructions. To add a facing to the top edge (neckline or waistline), see Neckline Facings (page 71) or Waistline Facings for Zippers (page 108).

NOTE

A specialized invisible zipper foot made for your sewing machine will give you the best result. It's sometimes possible to use a narrow zipper foot that allows you to stitch very close to the zipper chain/teeth, but a standard zipper foot is completely unsuitable if the foot extends behind or in front of the needle position.

Inserting an Invisible Zipper

My example here uses a neckline facing, and I will refer to the CB seam and neckline edge—it makes the language simpler—but the process is exactly the same on a waistline or any other seam.

1. Construct the garment to the point where the CB seam is about to be sewn. Finish the edges of the CB seam allowances separately, but don't sew the seam.

2. On the wrong side of the zipper (where you can see the zipper chain), make chalk marks on both sides of the tape, level with the ends of the top and bottom stoppers (the hard plastic bits).

Also mark both sides of the tape at the midway point of the zipper length.

3. Place the garment right side out on your work surface, with the 2 CB edges facing each other and top and bottom edges aligned. On the right side of the fabric, mark both CB seam allowances with a chalk pencil (or disappearing fabric marker) to show the depth of the neckline seam allowance.

4. Place the zipper facedown, aligning the top stopper marks on the zipper tape with these marks on the CB seam allowance. Smoothing the zipper tape flat to the fabric, mark the midway and bottom stopper positions on both CB seam allowances. These alignment points will help you to sew the zipper in evenly and without puckering.

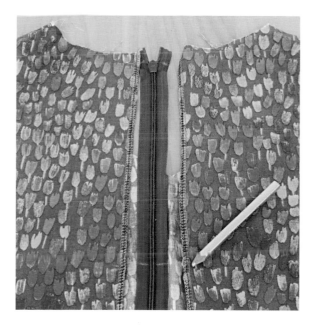

5. With the right side of the zipper to the right side of the fabric, match a zipper tape to the finished edge of the CB seam allowance, as shown (above right). Align the zipper tape marks

with the marks on the seam allowance. Open the zipper all the way, and pin it in place at 1 or 2 points, if necessary.

Tip To make it easier to hold the zipper while you sew, you can stitch it in place on the edge of the seam allowance using the standard presser foot or the normal zipper foot.

6. Sew the zipper in place using an invisible zipper foot, with the zipper chain traveling through the groove that is farthest from the edge of the tape you are stitching. (If you have only a normal narrow zipper foot, try to stitch as close as you can to the zipper chain/teeth.) Stitch as far as you can down toward the base of the zipper. Stop and backstitch as soon as the presser foot touches the zipper pull.

7. With the right sides of the garment together, match the other side of the zipper to the other CB seam allowance, aligning the marks with those on the zipper tape. Open the zipper and stitch it in place until the presser foot touches the zipper head.

Tips • *To make it easier to get going, start ¾" (2 cm) from the top, with the zipper foot on the uncurled zipper chain. Reverse sew back to the start of the tape and then stitch forward.*

• *As you sew, keep tension on the zipper tape, holding it in front of and behind the needle as it moves at its own pace through the machine.*

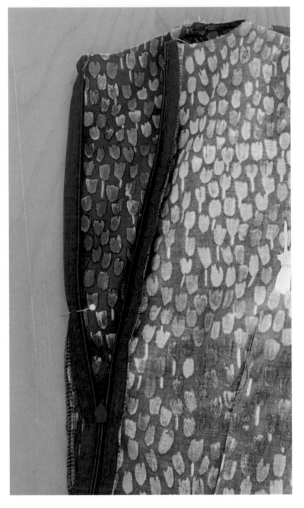

8. Close the zipper and align the rest of the CB seam, pulling the unattached zipper end out of the way. Using a standard zipper foot (*not* the invisible zipper foot), backstitch and begin the CB seam at the base of the zipper, at the full seam allowance depth (which will be slightly wider than the seam allowance for the zipper). Continue to sew the CB seam to the bottom of the garment pieces; you can change to a normal foot for this.

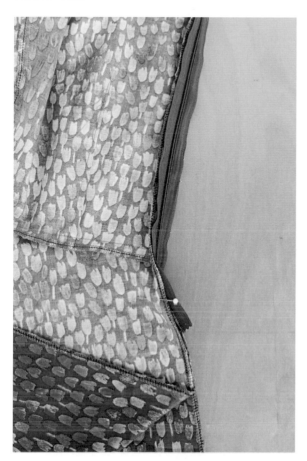

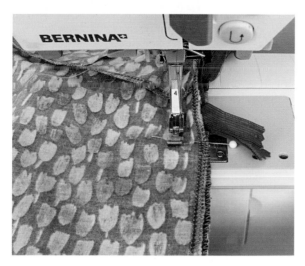

9. Press the CB seam allowances open.

10. Attach the standard zipper foot to the machine again. Stitching as close to the zipper chain as possible, sew each side of the zipper tape to the seam allowances.

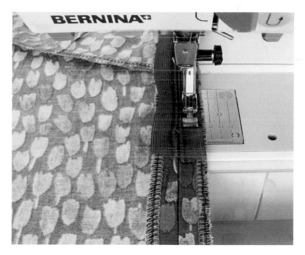

You can now attach a waistband (page 104) or facing (page 88) to your garment.

NOTE

An invisible zipper may be in the waist-to-hip area of a side seam or the CB seam of a dress without an opening at the top of the garment. Insert the zipper in the same way, but sew the seam both above and below the zipper instead of only below it.

Again, these instructions are for a CB opening and neckline facing, but the process can be applied to any seam and faced edge.

1. Construct a facing for the garment (see Neckline Facings, page 71, or Waistline Facings for Zippers, page 108); then cut and sew the facing. The seam allowances on the zipper ends of the facing need to be ¼″ (6 mm). Check your pattern and trim them to this width if necessary.

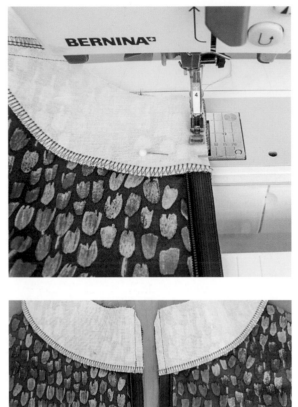

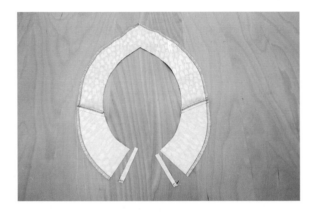

2. Open the zipper on the garment. Place the facing and garment right sides together, aligning the CB ends of the facing with the edges of the zipper tape and the CB seam allowances (the zipper will be sandwiched in between).

3. Using the standard zipper foot, stitch each end of the facing in place with a ¼″ (6 mm) seam allowance. At the top of the zipper, trim the seam allowance (including the zipper tape) at an angle to reduce bulk.

4. Still keeping the right sides together, match the shoulder seams of the garment and facing together and align the neckline edges toward the zipper. The facing will appear slightly too short (it's not). Fold the seam allowances of the facing and zipper flat against the facing. The fabric of the garment will be folded level with the CB notches, and the chain of the zipper will be inside the fold. The facing seam will be ¼″ (6 mm) in from the folded edge. Pin the facing in this position.

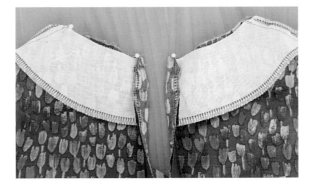

5. Backstitching at both ends, stitch the full length of the neckline; then understitch the facing (page 30).

NOTE

On a V-neck, snip into the corner point to allow the shape to turn through. If you can't understitch all the way around the point without causing puckers, stop and backstitch; then start again on the other side of the V.

6. Trim or pink the excess seam allowance to about ⅛" (3 mm) from the stitching. Turn and press the facing in place on the inside of the garment, using the understitched edge to push the seam out to the very edge. You'll see that the facing sits very neatly ¼" (6 mm) behind the chain of the zipper, making a neat finish at the corner.

 You might choose to topstitch ¼"–⅜" (6–10 mm) from the edge of the garment.

7. To hold the facing in place, discreetly backstitch the edge of the facing to the shoulder seam allowances without catching the outer garment in the stitch.

LAPPED ZIPPER

Skill Level: Intermediate

A lapped zipper is a classic method of inserting a standard dress or skirt zipper. You can add one to any seam if you make the seam allowances ⅝″ (1.5 cm). To convert from a button closure at the CF or CB, remove the button extension from the original pattern before you add the seam allowance. To change an invisible zipper to a lapped zipper, widen the seam allowance by ¼″ (6 mm).

Lapped Zipper for a Waistband Finish   *Skill Level: Intermediate*

1. Cut the garment pieces. Finish the edges of the CB seam allowances separately, and press them flat. Measure the length of the zipper from the top of the tape to the bottom stopper, and mark this distance on the seam allowance of the garment. Notch the CB at the ⅝″ (1.5 cm) seam allowance depth at the top of the seam.

2. Sew the CB seam from the bottom stopper mark to the bottom of the garment piece, backstitching at each end.

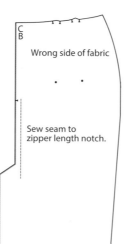

C
B

Wrong side of fabric

Sew seam to zipper length notch.

3. Press the seam open below the opening for the zipper. On the overlap side (the right-hand side from the wrong side of the fabric), fold and press the ⅝″ (1.5 cm) seam allowance, continuing up from the end of the seam in a smooth line.

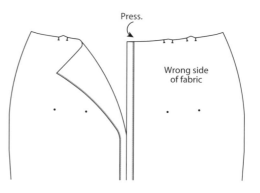

Press.

Wrong side of fabric

Tip — *To make it easier to sew an accurate ⅝″ (1.5 cm) seam below the zipper, you can press this crease before sewing the CB seam. Use the crease as a stitch guide as you sew the seam, beginning at the notch that marks the bottom stopper of the zipper.*

4. On the underlap side (the left-hand side from the wrong side of the fabric), fold the seam allowance ½″ (12 mm) from the edge and press a crease. This crease will be ⅛″ (3 mm) beyond the seam, forming the underlap extension.

Tip *Fuse ¼" (6 mm) fusible tape, keeping a scant ¼" (5 mm) from the edge of the seam allowance. Use the backing paper as an edge to turn the seam allowance and press a sharp crease. Remove the backing paper to make it easy to hold the zipper in place.*

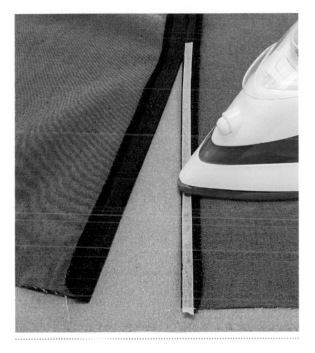

5. With the garment right side up, place the zipper right side up behind the extended underlap. Align the folded edge with the edge of the zipper teeth. Fuse it in place.

NOTE
If you are making the lapped zipper with a facing, return to Insert the Zipper, Step 3 (page 93) now.

6. Using a zipper foot, edgestitch a generous ¹⁄₁₆" (2 mm) from the fold to attach the zipper.

NOTES ON SEWING ZIPPERS

- *Always use a zipper foot, with the needle on the side that is closest to the teeth/chain of the zipper.*

- *Never try to sew around the zipper pull. Stop with the needle down and the presser foot raised, and move the pull out of the way (opening or closing the zipper) as you stitch the length of the zipper.*

7. Press fusible tape to the other side of the zipper and remove the backing paper. Align the overlapping side of the garment over the zipper, matching the folded edge to the seam allowance depth notch at the top of the underlap, and press it flat.

8. Feel the zipper chain beneath the right side of the fabric, and run a thumbnail or Hera marker along its edge on the overlap side. Unzip the zipper halfway and then realign the overlap. Use tape to hold the overlap in place, with one edge of the tape following the thumbnail stitch guide.

Cut the tape square across at the bottom of the zipper opening.

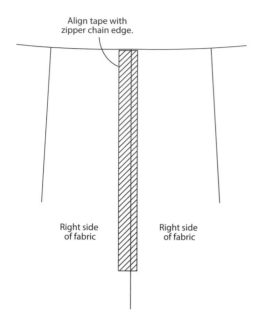

9. Stitching around the tape (not through it), topstitch through the fabric of the garment and seam allowance to attach it to the zipper underneath. Open and readjust the tape to move the zipper pull to the top; then sew along the rest of the zipper's length. Pivot and stitch across the bottom end of the tape, backstitching securely. Remove the tape, and press to set the stitches into the fabric. Marvel at your lovely zipper, and attach a waistband (page 104).

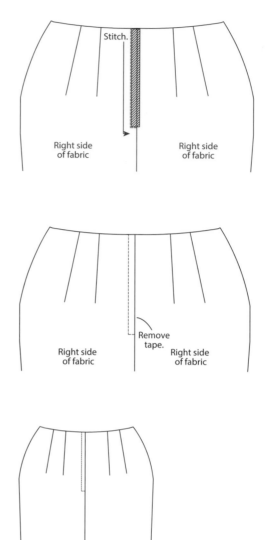

Lapped Zipper with a Facing   *Skill Level: Intermediate to Confident*

On most garments with a neckline or waistline facing, I prefer to use an invisible zipper, but it's not always possible (last-minute late-night sewing, when only the zippers in my stash are available ... you know the story). This production method is a handy technique to know for such occasions and also serves as an alternative to the domestic methods that many patterns with a lapped zipper and facing use. It gives a very neat and professional finish.

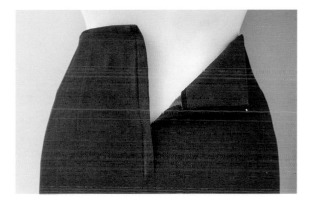

PREPARATION

1. The seam allowance on the zippered edge needs to be ⅝″ (1.5 cm). Change it on the garment pattern, if necessary, and notch the length of the zipper from the top of the tape to the bottom stopper. Also notch the seam allowance width at the top edge of the pattern piece. Cut the garment pieces.

2. Prepare a facing pattern for the waistline (see Waistline Facings for Zippers, page 108) or neckline (see Neckline Facings, page 71), adding a ⅝″ (1.5 cm) seam allowance at the edge that will attach to the zipper and allowances to match the garment on all the other seams. Block fuse interfacing (page 33), and cut the facings.

3. Sew the seams to join the front and back facings together. Peel back the interfacing from the seam allowances and trim it off; then serge the seam allowance edges.

4. With the right side facing up, place the facing on the cutting mat with the CB edges toward you. Trim ½″ (12 mm) off the end of the facing on the left-hand side. Trim ¾″ (2 cm) from the end on the right-hand side.

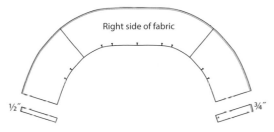

INSERT THE ZIPPER

1. Construct the garment to the point where the front is joined to the back. Staystitch (page 29) the waistline as necessary. (I don't staystitch stable denim, as shown here.)

2. Serge, seam, and press the CB seam allowances in the same way as in Lapped Zipper for a Waistband Finish, Steps 1–5 (page 90).

3. With the garment right side up, place the zipper right side up behind the extended underlap. Align the folded edge with the edge of the zipper teeth. Fuse or glue (don't pin or sew) the zipper in place.

4. Unfold the seam allowance so the zipper tape is flat against it. Turn the zipper to the underside. Using a zipper foot and moving the zipper head out of the way as you sew past it, stitch as close as you can to the crease in the seam allowance along the full length of the zipper tape.

5. Close the zipper. With the garment pieces right sides together and the overlap side to the top, align the CB notches on the waist/neckline edge. (The folded seam allowance on the overlap side matches to the CB notch on the underlap.) Pin along the inside of the crease in the seam allowance to hold it to the other garment piece.

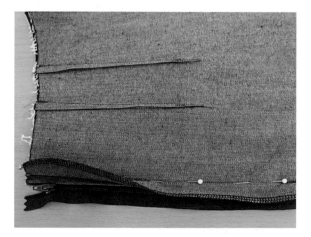

6. Unfold the overlap side's seam allowance completely on top of the zipper tape. The unattached zipper tape naturally sits in its final position against the seam allowance. Stitch it in place here, as close to the zipper chain as you can. Remove the pins as you sew, and move the zipper head out of the way.

Tips • *Instead of pinning, fuse or glue the tape in place on the seam allowance, moving the zipper head out of the way so you can attach the top of the zipper.*

• *Sew the zipper in place from the bottom end upward so the last thing you have to do is move the zipper head.*

7. With the right sides of the fabric together, match the facing to the top edge of the garment. Align and pin only the side/shoulder seams of the garment and facing together. The facing will look too short to fit to the zippered edges, but it is correct.

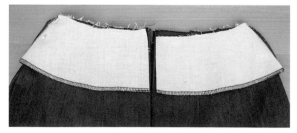

8. Match the ends of the facing to the seam allowances of the garment at the zipper opening (the zipper tape may overhang the edges), and stitch with a ¼″ (6 mm) seam allowance, back-stitching at each end.

9. Match the facing to the complete neck/waist-line edge, allowing the fabric of the garment to roll over the zipper with the seam allowances sitting a little in from the edge. On the overlap side, take care that the fabric folds at the CB seam allowance notch and on the underlap side that it folds tightly over the zipper teeth. The seam allowances will fold toward the facings.

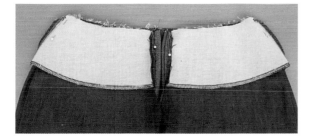

10. Backstitching on the folded ends, stitch around the neck/waistline seam of the garment.

11. Understitch, trim, and press the facings as per the invisible zipper neckline facing instructions (see Neckline Facing and Button Closure, Sew and Attach the Facing, Steps 5–7, page 78) .

12. Follow the directions for topstitching the overlay side of the zipper (see Lapped Zipper for a Waistband Finish, Steps 7–9, pages 91 and 92). For best results, also stitch a hook-and-eye closure above the zipper (hook on the overlap, eye on the underlap).

ZIPPERED FLY
Skill Level: Intermediate

A pants pattern with a side or back zipper can be altered to make a zippered fly for a more street-savvy style.

Prepare the Pattern

1. Trace a draft copy of the pants pattern. Measure the CF seamline to the hip level (just above where the seamline curves to make the crotch) and place a dot. For waist-high adult pants, the mark is around 6″–7″ (15–18 cm) from the waistline edge; for low-rise pants and children's wear, it may be 4″ (10 cm) or less.

2. To make the fly facing, rule a line on the front draft parallel to the CF seam, 1″–1½″ (2.5–4 cm) from the seamline (narrower for children's wear, wider for adults). Square across to the dot on the CF. Curve the bottom end of the facing from the parallel line to about ⅜″–½″ (10–12 mm) below the notch.

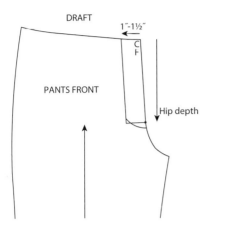

DRAFT

1″–1½″

C F

PANTS FRONT

Hip depth

3. Trace a pattern for the fly facing, adding ⅜″–½″ (10–12 mm) seam allowances all the way around. Notch the position of the CF on the waistline seam allowance, and place a straight-grain arrow parallel to the CF seam.

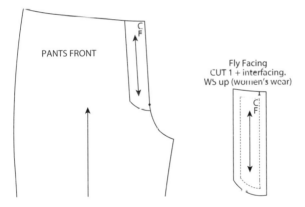

PANTS FRONT

C F

Fly Facing
CUT 1 + interfacing.
WS up (women's wear)

C F

The facing sits on the inside of the overlapping side of the fly front, with the right side of the facing visible on the inside of the garment (see Overwraps and Underlaps, page 27). Label the pattern with right side (RS) or wrong side (WS) so that the pattern is cut out with the correct side of the fabric facing up.

4. For the fly shield that sits on the inside of the zipper against the body, trace the facing shape with the shorter length on the fold. Add seam allowances to match the other pieces all the way around, except add ¼″ (6 mm) to the curved bottom edge. Notch the seam allowance level with the dot on the CF, and place the straight-grain arrow on the fold line.

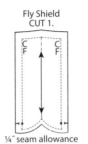

Fly Shield
CUT 1.

C F   C F

¼″ seam allowance

5. Trace a pattern for the pants, adding seam allowances all the way around. Parallel to the CF between the waistline and the bottom edge of the facing, draw an extension ¼″ (6 mm) for children's wear or ⅜″ (10 mm) for adults from the seam allowance. Notch the CF position on the waistline edge and level with the dot on the CF seam.

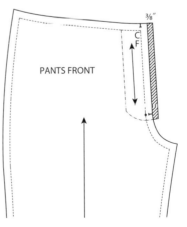

⅜″

C F

PANTS FRONT

6. Make a waistband (page 104) for the pants, adding the width of the fly facing to the waist measurement on the underlap side.

Cut and Sew the Fly Facing

1. Cut out the garment, 1 fly shield, and 1 facing piece from the selected fabric. Snip all the notches and mark the dots on the wrong side of the fabric.

2. Cut interfacing for the fly facing, and fuse it to the wrong side of the fabric. Fold the fly shield pattern in half lengthwise, and cut interfacing to that size. Trim the seam allowances off the curved bottom edge of the interfacing, and fuse it to the wrong side of one-half of the fly shield.

3. On the overlap side of the pants front, trim off the extension at the CF, and serge the (crotch) seam allowance, beginning at the notch. On the underlap side, serge the extension and the crotch seam allowances.

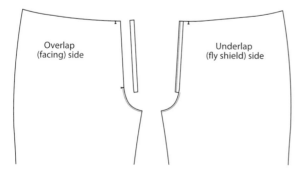

Overlap (facing) side

Underlap (fly shield) side

4. Sew any pockets, darts, or other details to the garment pieces before making the fly front. If you are making women's pants, match the backs to the fronts, and then sew and serge the inner leg and side seams.

NOTE

Traditionally, jeans and men's trousers are made with the front and back crotch seams sewn separately; the fly is inserted and then the inner leg seam is sewn from hemline (over the crotch seam) to hemline. For women's wear, the backs of the pants are attached to the fronts first and the crotch seam is sewn from front to back (over the inner leg seams) before the fly is inserted.

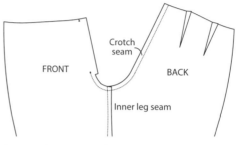

Crotch seam

FRONT

BACK

Inner leg seam

A women's wear crotch seam

For ease and clarity in photography, these images show how to make the fly when working only on the fronts of the garment (men's method). It is exactly the same method as when the full crotch seam is sewn.

5. Place the garment fronts right sides together. Align and pin the dot markings below the fly opening. Sew the crotch seam, backstitching at both ends and stopping at the pin. If you are sewing the (women's wear) crotch seam, also serge the back crotch seam allowances together.

CF

Pants front
Wrong side of fabric

NOTE

Alternatively, you can reverse the order of Steps 3 and 4 (at left) and serge the full length of the crotch seam after the inner leg seams are sewn. The back crotch seam can then be seamed and pressed open.

6. Fold the fly shield in half lengthwise, right sides together, and stitch the ¼″ (6 mm) seam on the curved bottom edge. Pink the seam allowance to reduce bulk, and turn the shield through to the right side. Press it flat, draw a chalk mark level with the zipper length notch, and serge the CF seam allowances together.

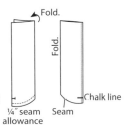

7. To ensure that you're working on the right side of the fly shield, place the underlap side of the garment right side up, and then place the fly shield with the serged edge toward the CF extension. Place the zipper right side up on the fly extension, aligning the edge of the zipper tape ⅛″ (3 mm) in from the serged edge of the shield and the bottom stopper level with the chalk line. Use fusible tape to hold the zipper tape in place if necessary, and stitch ¼″ (6 mm) from the edge of the tape.

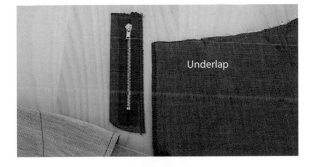

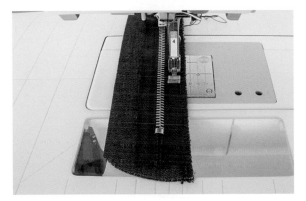

8. With right sides together, place the fly shield on the garment front, aligning the serged edge of the fly shield with the zipper extension. Stitch ⅜″ (10 mm) from the edge along the length of the extension. The stitches should cover the line of stitching on the zipper tape.

Tip

To avoid having to sew around the zipper head, start with the zipper open, and stop sewing about halfway along. Lower the needle and raise the presser foot to close the zipper before stitching the other half of the zipper length.

9. Turn the fly shield to the right side. Backstitching at each end, edgestitch the full length of the fly shield on the garment side of the seam.

10. Serge around the curved outer edge of the fly facing. With right sides together, match the fly facing with the other garment front, aligning the seam allowances and CF notches. Stitch from the CF notch to the dot marking, backstitching at both ends.

12. Place the garment right side up on your work surface. At the waistline, align the CF edge of the overlap with the CF notch on the underlap side of the garment. Pin vertically along the CF edge to hold it in place.

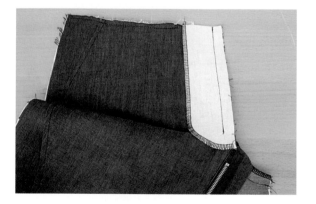

11. Understitch (page 30) the seam allowances to the facing side a generous ⅟₁₆″ (2 mm) from the seam. Turn the facing to the inside of the garment piece and press it flat.

13. From the wrong side of the garment, lift the fly shield but leave the zipper tape against the fly facing.

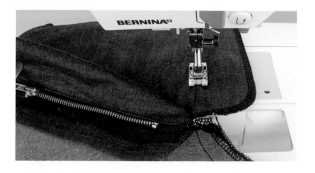

14. Use fusible tape to hold the zipper tape in place against the facing.

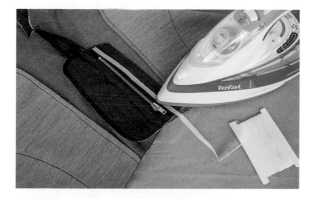

15. Lift the facing and stitch the zipper tape to it (but not through to the front of the garment) ⅛″ (3 mm) from the teeth of the zipper.

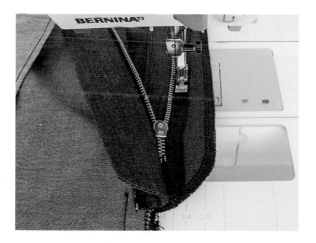

16. Use a Hera marker and ruler to mark the stitch line of the fly front on the overlap side of the garment. Pin the facing in place on the back of the garment front, folding the fly shield

out of the way. From the right side of the fabric, stitch along the marker line to the point where the facing curves, moving the zipper head out of the way (open and close the zipper) as you sew past it. Backstitch and cut the thread.

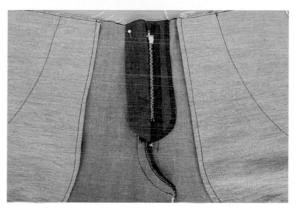

17. Close the zipper and pin the fly shield back in place behind the facing. Stitch the curve at the bottom of the fly through all the layers, backstitching neatly at both ends.

Waistlines

If you have a skirt or pants pattern that has a facing at the waist, you can easily change it to a waistband or vice versa.

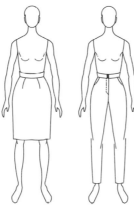

Waistbands   Facings

WAISTBANDS
Skill Level: Basic

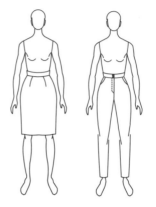

Prepare the Pattern

1. Take note of which seam will have the zippered or button opening on the garment: CB, CF, or side seam. Decide on the width of the waistband. It should be somewhere between 1″ and 2″ (2.5 cm and 5 cm).

2. Measure the waist stitch line on both the front and back pattern pieces, not including any of the darts or seam allowances. Add the measurements together and record the half-waist measurement. Double this and record the full waist measurement.

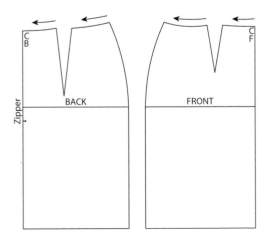

3. Draw a straight horizontal line the length of the full waist measurement. At each end, square up to draw a line twice the width of the desired waistband. Label both vertical lines with the position of the zipper opening: CF, CB, or side seam. Measure and mark the halfway point on the waistband. If the zipper opening is at the CB, then this will be the CF, and vice versa.

4. Extend the horizontal line 1½″ (4 cm) from one end of the waistband for the underwrap, and square up.

NOTE

For a garment with a fly front (page 96), the underwrap needs to be the same width as the fly shield.

5. Draw the other side of the waistband at the top of the vertical lines (at 2 × the width of the desired waistband). Add seam allowances to match those of the garment around all the edges, and notch the vertical lines on the pattern. Draw a straight-grain arrow along the center horizontal line.

Height = 2 × finished width of waistband

Add seam allowances and notches.

Cut and Fuse the Waistband

1. Cut the waistband on the straight grain and snip the notches. Cut the interfacing (without the seam allowance or for only 1 side if you need to reduce bulk), and fuse it to the wrong side of the waistband.

2. On the wrong side of the waistband, draw a chalk line to join the 2 notches that mark the underwrap.

NOTE

To check which way up it will be sewn, place one side of the waistband (all right sides facing out, as if it has been sewn on) around the top of the garment, aligning the chalk line on the waistband with the edge of the underlap side of the garment (or with the seam of the fly shield on a fly front). The top half of the waistband will be folded to the inside of the garment.

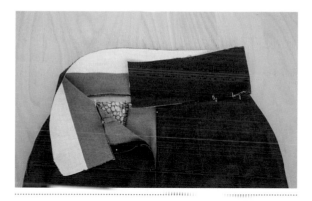

Attach the Waistband to the Garment

1. Construct the garment to the point where the waistband needs to be attached. Staystitch the waist seamline.

2. Finish the raw edges on the inside of the waistband with serging (page 14) or binding (page 35). If you are binding the edge, do so

only between the overwrap seam allowance and ⅝″ (1.5 cm) over the notch that marks the underwrap. Serging can include the overwrap seam allowance.

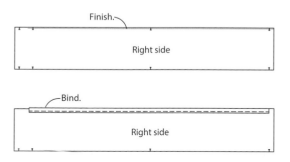

NOTE

If you want the inside edge of the waistband to be turned under (like on jeans), you can leave this step until after the waistband is attached.

3. With right sides together, match the waistband to the waistline edge of the garment, aligning the corresponding seams and notches.

NOTE

The underwrap on the waistband will extend beyond the edge of the garment, but only the seam allowance will extend beyond the garment on the overwrap end of the waistband.

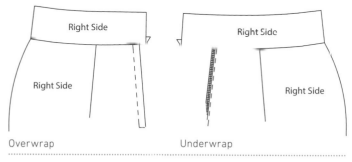

4. With the waistband on top (to allow the feed dogs to ease the garment fabric), stitch the waistband to the garment with the required seam allowance, backstitching securely at both ends.

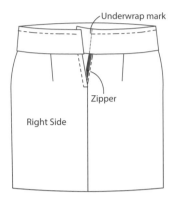

5. With the right sides of the fabric together, fold the waistband in half lengthwise, aligning the raw edges at the short ends of the waistband. On the underwrap end of the waistband, match the ends of the chalk line together and pin them.

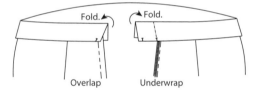

6. On the overwrapping side of the waistband (or on both sides of a fly front), fold the (seamed) waistline seam allowances up toward the waistband. The inside edge of the waistband will sit flat against the right side of the garment, with the seam allowance extending below the waistline seam. Stitch across the end of the waistband, backstitching securely at both ends of the seam.

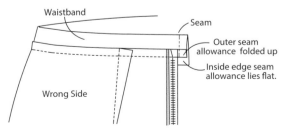

7. If the waistband underwrap extends onto a zipper shield (on a fly front, page 96), it will be sewn in the same manner as the overwrap (see Step 6, below left). If it extends, as shown, beyond the edge of the garment (as it will on a lapped [page 90] or invisible [page 84] zipper opening), stitch along the bottom edge, keeping the seam allowances accurate, and stop at the chalk line. Backstitch securely without accidentally stitching onto the fabric of the garment.

8. Trim the corners of the seam allowance to reduce bulk; then fold and finger-press them back onto the waistband. Stitch across the short ends of the underwrap.

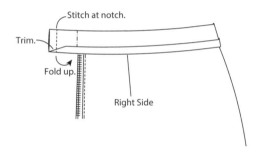

Tip *On very bulky fabric, stitch the underwrap with a single seam, pivoting on the corner, and then trim off the excess seam allowance.*

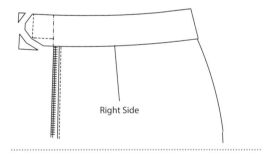

9. Turn the waistband to the right side. At the zipper ends, tuck the corner of the seam allowance into the waistband with a neat diagonal fold. You may have to clip a little of the corner seam allowance to reduce bulk.

Before you turn through the corner of the waistband, fold the corner of the inner waistband up, and then tuck it and all the waistband seam allowances behind those of the garment (and zipper) waistline. Hold them in place as you turn the waistband through, and it will all sit very flat and neatly.

10. From the right side of the garment, carefully align, fold, and press to create a waistband that is an even width around its full length. Pin or fuse the inner waistband to the waist seam.

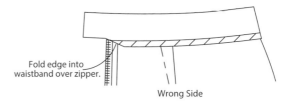

Fold edge into waistband over zipper.

Wrong Side

If you want to turn the seam allowance under on the inside of the waistband, press it under with the folded edge sitting a generous $\frac{1}{16}$" (2 mm) below the waistline seam. Fuse or pin from the right side of the garment to hold the inner waistband in place.

11. Working on the right side of the garment, stitch-in-the-ditch of the seam to catch the inside waistband to the back of the waistline seam.

NOTE

An edgestitching presser foot can make this process very easy. If you don't have one, work slowly along the seam, gently flattening and opening the seam with both hands as you sew.

WAISTLINE FACINGS FOR ZIPPERS

Skill Level: Intermediate

If you have a skirt or pants pattern with a waistband, you can remove the waistband from the design. This creates a comfortable low-waisted garment with very simple, flattering design lines.

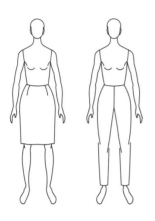

Prepare the Pattern

1. Trace a draft of the garment pattern without seam allowances or button/fly extensions.

NOTES

- *As a starting point, work with an invisible or lapped zipper opening, not a fly or buttoned front. (Both of these are possible but are more complicated to sew.) I'd recommend a CB placement for your first attempt. These instructions are for a CB placement, and once you learn the process, you can use the method in other positions.*

- *Inseam or patch pockets are easier to manage with a facing than a cutaway hip-pocket style. You can remove hip pockets from the pattern before making a change to the waistline (see the note in Hip Pockets, page 43).*

- *Removing a curved waistband or yoke is a little more complex than removing a straight one. You need to trace the draft of the waistband or yoke pieces and place these pieces back on the top edge of the garment draft. You may also have to slash vertically through a wide yoke draft to match its bottom edge to the garment draft. The top edge of the yoke will open up, and the slash lines will become darts in your garment piece. This is basically a reversal of the following process for making a facing from a darted waistline. If you're a beginner, begin with a straight waistband.*

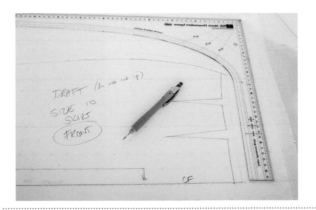

2. A waistline facing needs to be wide enough to stabilize the top section of the garment: 1″–2″ (2.5–5 cm) for children's wear or 2″–4″ (5–10 cm) for adult sizes. Measure your chosen facing depth at several points below the waistline edge on both the front and back drafts. Use a curved ruler to rule lines parallel to the top edge of the garment, connecting these points on each draft. Figure A

3. If there are no darts in the garment pattern, you can skip to Waistline Facings for Zippers, Trace the Pattern, Step 1 (page 111). If the pattern has darts, trace the section between the side seam and the first dart, with the facing depth line as the bottom edge. Figure B

4. Move the paper to align the dart line of the first section on the other side of the dart, and then trace off the next section of the facing. Figure C

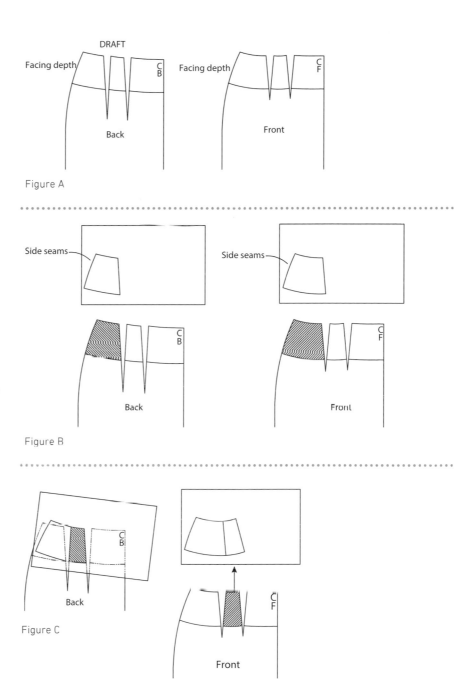

DRAFT

Facing depth

Back

C B

Facing depth

Front

C F

Figure A

Side seams

Side seams

Back

C B

Front

C F

Figure B

Back

C B

Front

C F

Figure C

5. Repeating Step 4 for as many darts as are within the design line area, trace off the rest of the facing patterns. Clearly mark the CF, CB, and side seams, and draw grainlines parallel to the CF and the CB.

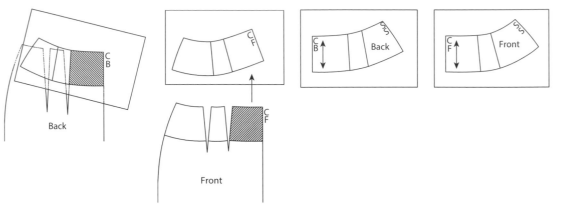

6. Smooth (see Proving or Trueing a Line, page 25) the points of any darts to make a smooth line on the facing; then trace the trued lines back onto the garment draft, matching each facing segment to the darts.

Trace the Pattern

1. Trace the garment pieces from waistline to hem, including the darts and any pocket or surface details. You don't need to mark in the facing line. Draw the grainlines, and label the pieces with cutting instructions. Draw an "on fold" symbol at the CF.

2. If you're planning to use an invisible zipper, add a CB seam allowance of ½″ (12 mm). For a lapped zipper, add ⅝″ (1.5 cm). Measuring down from the waistline seam, notch the length of the zipper you want to use on the outer edge of the CB seam allowance.

NOTE

A standard length for a waist zipper is 7″ (18 cm), but if you have wide hips and a narrow waist, you can use an 8″ or 9″ (20 cm or 23 cm) zipper to take the strain off the garment when you're dressing.

3. Add your preferred seam allowances around all the other edges but *not* to the area between the darts. Notch the position of the CB seamline at the top of the waistline seam allowance.

4. Before you cut out the paper patterns, fold the darts so the excess paper is facing toward the CB. Use tape if necessary to hold the pattern flat over the dart, and cut along the edge of the waistline seam allowance. Open out the pattern again (remove or cut through the tape), and you will see that the outside edge of the dart pick-up is the correct shape to fold into position when the garment is sewn. Notch where the darts finish on the outer edges of the seam allowance, and put a dot marking on the vanishing point of each dart.

5. Take the facing patterns that you traced from the draft and, along the waistline and side seam edges, add the same seam allowances as on the garment. Draw an "on fold" symbol at the CF, or trace a full pattern from the half-pattern (page 22).

6. At the CB seam of the facing, add a ¼″ (6 mm) seam allowance for an invisible zipper or a ⅝″ (1.5 cm) seam allowance for a lapped zipper. You don't need to add anything to the bottom of the facing, as this will simply be finished with a serged or bound edge.

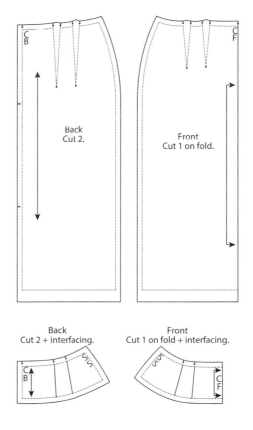

Sew the Facing

1. Block fuse (page 33) interfacing to the fabric, and cut 1 front facing (CF on the fold) and 1 pair of back facings from the interfaced fabric.

2. With the right sides of the fabric together, match the side seams of the facing pieces to join the back pieces to the fronts. Be careful not to confuse the CB with a side seam. Stitch the side seams with an accurate seam allowance, and backstitch securely at each end.

3. Finish the seam allowances (open or closed); then clip the waistline ends at an angle to reduce bulk. Press the facing seams open or toward the front.

4. Serge or bind the facing's bottom edge (see Attaching Binding to Seam-Allowance Edges, page 35). You are now ready to attach the facing to the garment (see Invisible Zipper, page 84, or Lapped Zipper with a Facing, page 93).

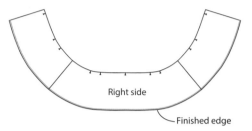

Right side

Finished edge

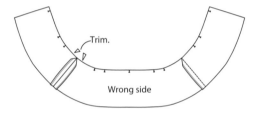

Trim.

Wrong side

ATTACHING A SKIRT WITH A FOLDED BUTTON FACING

Skill Level: Basic

If you have altered a dress pattern to add a center front button closure, here is how to attach the altered skirt.

1. Sew the skirt side seams and serge the edges.

2. With the right sides of the fabric together, match the skirt and bodice along the waistline seam, wrapping the facing around the button extension edge of the bodice. Sew the waistline seam, backstitching securely at each end. Serge the seam.

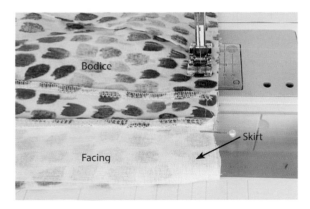

3. Turn the skirt facing through to the right side of the fabric, and press a crease along the fold. The skirt is now ready for the hem, buttons, and buttonholes.

Classic Shirt Yokes

A shirt yoke runs over the shoulders and across the top section of the shirt back with two layers of fabric—cut with the straight (strongest) grain running across the width—giving support to the shape and fall of the garment.

The seam between the shirt back and yoke can create shaping around the back and shoulders without the need for darts. Extra movement can be added in the back of the shirt with pleats and gathers below the yoke.

The width of the yoke depends upon the size of the garment and the styling—a classic men's dress shirt usually has a yoke depth of around 2″ (5 cm), but on casual shirts or women's wear it can be wherever you want it to be. Look at existing garments or make a muslin test garment, and draw in where you would like the bottom of the yoke to be.

YOKE ON A PATTERN WITH A SHOULDER DART

Skill Level: Basic to Intermediate

To make a yoke on a fitted shirt or dress bodice, you need to "close out" the shoulder dart first.

1. Trace a draft of the garment back and front, and add the button placket or facing details to the draft (page 57). Measure the desired depth of the yoke down from the back shoulder point, and square across from the armhole line to the shoulder dart. It's best if the bottom of the dart is on, or within ¼" (6 mm) of, the yoke line. If it's within ¼" (6 mm), you can simply change the length of the dart to match the yoke.

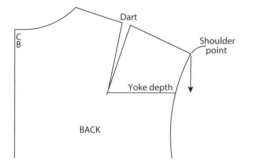

2. Trace the outer yoke section (between the armhole and the dart), and then pivot it to align the traced section with the other side of the dart. A new dart shape will open up from the armhole edge.

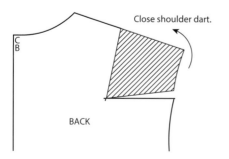

3. Square across from the yoke depth on the armhole to the CB line to form the bottom edge of the yoke. Draw a line from where the bottom of the original shoulder dart crosses the new yoke line to the lower corner of the armhole dart shape, reshaping the dart to finish on the yoke line.

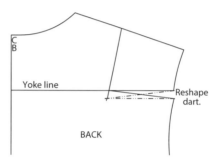

4. You can rule a gentle curve with a curved ruler to smooth out the angle. Measure the line across the bottom of the yoke and then the line at the top of the shirt back. If the shirt back is more than ¼" (6 mm) longer than the yoke, change the shape of the curve slightly to match it.

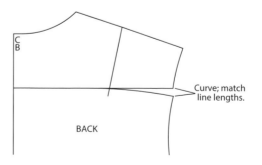

5. Continue creating the yoke draft and pattern, following from Step 2 in Yoke on a Dartless Pattern (next page).

Yoke on a Dartless Pattern   *Skill Level: Basic*

1. Trace a draft of the shirt back and front. On the back, measure the depth of the yoke down from the armhole edge of the shoulder seam and square across to the CB line.

onto the back draft, smoothing the neckline and armhole curves over the joins.

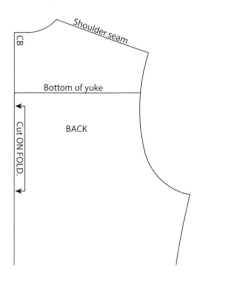

2. On the front draft, measure and rule a parallel line ¾″ (2 cm) in from the shoulder seam.

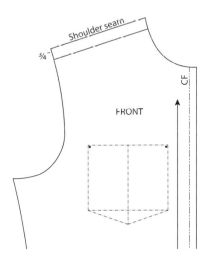

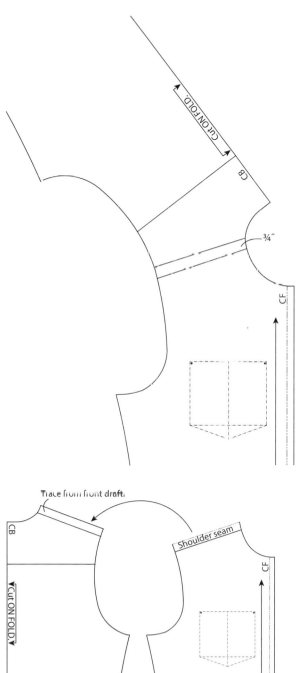

Place the back draft over the front, matching the drafts along the shoulder seam, and trace the ¾″-wide (2 cm-wide) strip from the front

3. You can add 1 or 2 pleats or gathers to allow for more movement in the back of the shirt. Rule a line parallel to the CB line at least ¾″ (2 cm) outside the CB. This can be a box pleat (or a section of gathering) at the CB, or you can mark a point in the middle of each shoulder blade area to make a knife pleat.

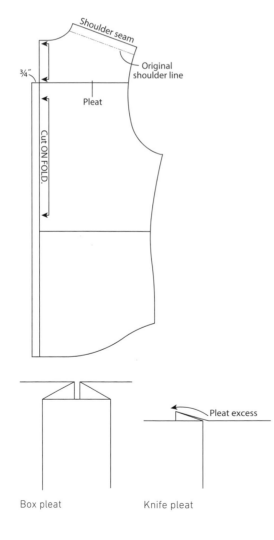

Box pleat   Knife pleat

4. Trace a full pattern from the yoke draft with the CB on the fold (page 22). Trace the new shoulder line (which was transferred from the front draft) as the front edge of the yoke, notching the original shoulder position on the neckline and armhole edges. Notch the CB on the neckline edge of the yoke, and notch any pleat positions. Add seam allowances (page 26) to all the edges. The neckline edge may have ¼″ (6 mm) seams (to match the collar seam allowance); otherwise, all seam allowances are ½″ (12 mm). Rule the straight grainline at a right angle to the CB line.

NOTE

Traditionally, a yoke is one piece (with the CB on the fold). But you can choose to make a two-piece yoke with a CB seam if you want to have the shoulder seams on the straight of grain (for example, to have stripes running parallel to the shoulder seam) or for more efficient cutting from your fabric (smaller pattern pieces being easier to slot in between other pattern pieces on the fabric). For a two-piece yoke, label the pattern "Cut 2 pairs" (or "Cut 4"), and add a seam allowance on the CB edge.

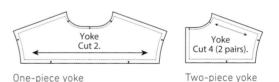

One-piece yoke   Two-piece yoke

5. Trace a pattern for the shirt back (not including the yoke area). You can make the back pattern to be "on fold" at CB or make a full pattern (page 22). Add seam allowances to all edges. Transfer all the notch points from the draft to the pattern, including the pleat placement. If the pleats are on the shoulder blades, notch the pleat width from the original pleat placement notch toward the CB. For a CB pleat, notch the position of the pleat extension as it is on the draft.

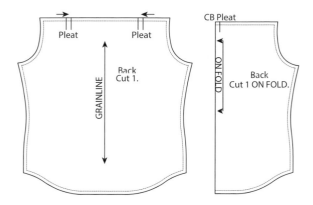

6. Trace the front pattern to the new shoulder line; don't include the section that was moved to the back. Add the button placket or facing details, and then add seam allowances all the way around the pattern piece, making sure they correspond with the seam allowances on the back and yoke. Transfer all darts, notches, and pocket placements onto the pattern, and place a lengthwise grainline arrow parallel to the CF.

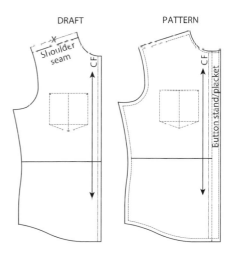

Attach the Yoke to the Shirt Back

1. Cut the garment pieces, including a shirt back, a pair of fronts, and 2 yokes (or 4 of the 2-piece yokes). Sew all darts, button stands, plackets, and pockets on the garment pieces. If you're using a 2-piece yoke, sew the CB seams

and press the seam allowances open. If you're attaching a convertible collar or Peter Pan collar with a neckline facing, see Attach the Collar, A Shirt with a Yoke (page 141) for the construction process for the yoke and collar. Otherwise, proceed.

2. With right sides together, align the bottom edge of the outer yoke with the top edge of the shirt back. Place the other (inner) yoke piece on the other side, with the right side of the yoke to the wrong side of the shirt back, and align all 3 yoke seam edges. Backstitching at both ends, seam them together with a ½″ (12 mm) seam.

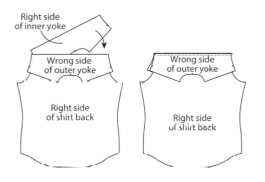

If you have trouble keeping all three layers aligned, stitch one yoke in place and then the other.

3. Flip the outer yoke up over the seam allowances and keep the inner yoke down. Holding all the seam allowances to the underside of the outer yoke, edgestitch or topstitch ⅟₁₆″–¼″ (2–6 mm) from the seam all the way across.

Yoke Shoulder Seams—Burrito Method *Skill Level: Basic*

1. With the right sides of the fabric together, align the shoulders of the shirt front and outer yoke. Stitch with a ½″ (12 mm) seam allowance, backstitching at both ends of the seam.

2. Roll up both front pieces and the back piece—from the hemlines to the yoke seamlines—so that they are all sitting on the right side of the outer yoke piece.

4. Pull the shirt pieces out through the neckline opening, and turn the yoke right side out. You will see that all the seams are completely concealed between the inner and outer yokes. Press the seams, and continue to construct the garment.

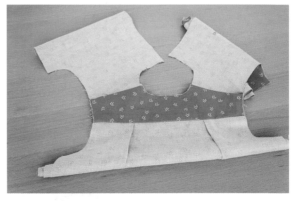

3. Fold the inner yoke around with the wrong side facing out, and sandwich the rolled-up garment pieces between the 2 yoke pieces. Align the shoulders of the inner yoke with the sewn shoulder seams, and then stitch over the seam, backstitching at each end.

Yoke Shoulder Seams—Production Style *Skill Level: Basic to Intermediate*

Once you have an understanding of the burrito method, you don't need to actually roll the garment pieces up to sew them.

1. Attach the yoke pieces to the back, as described in Yoke Shoulder Seams—Burrito Method, Steps 1–3 (page 120).

2. With the right sides of the fabric together, align the shoulder seamlines of the shirt front and outer yoke, and hold the seam allowances together. You can stitch this shoulder seam, but with practice you may be able to simply hold it and move on to the next step.

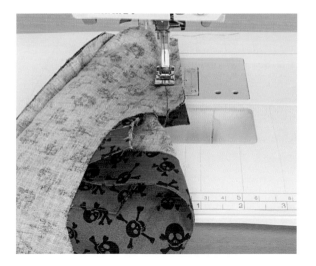

3. Allowing the body of the shirt to fall out from between the yoke pieces, fold the inner

yoke around to match the shoulder seamline to the shirt front. Carefully align the edges of all 3 seam allowances at the armhole end of the seam, and stitch the seam. The garment pieces will be quite scrunched up, so take care not to catch them in the seam.

4. Pull the garment pieces out of the yoke, and press the seams.

Collars

You can add or alter a collar on any shirt or bodice—changing the shape of an existing collar or changing a classic shirt collar to a casual convertible or feminine Peter Pan collar, or any variation of that exchange. In doing so, you'll change the whole look of the shirt.

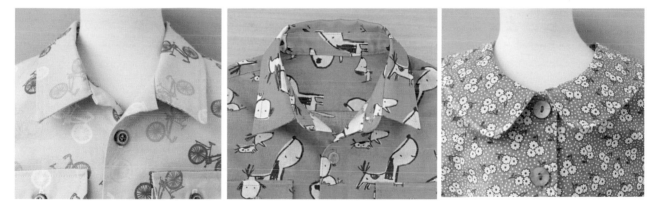

Convertible collar, collar and stand, and Peter Pan collar—all used on the same garment neckline

PREPARE THE GARMENT PATTERN

The first step is to have a neckline that fits comfortably around the neck. For a collar and stand or convertible collar, the neckline sits around the base of the neck. A Peter Pan collar can be on a high or low neckline.

If you have a shirt with a convertible collar or collar and stand, these collars are infinitely interchangeable. Leave the neckline on the pattern as it is, and move straight to Prepare the Collar Draft (below).

It's also possible to change a collarless garment pattern that has a low neckline to one that can accommodate a classic collar (see Raising a Low Neckline to Add a Collar, page 79).

PREPARE THE COLLAR DRAFT

This is how to begin creating both the convertible collar and classic collar and stand. Before you start, you will need a draft copy (without seam allowances) of your garment pattern, including a button extension (page 58) at the CF.

Tip — *Have a ready-made shirt that you like as a reference point when you are making a new collar pattern.*

1. Measure the neckline of the draft between the CB and the shoulder. Measure the front neckline between the shoulder and the button extension line. Write these measurements down separately, and then add them together and write down the total: the half-neckline measurement.

2. Rule a vertical line 4″–6″ (10–15 cm) long and label it "CB." From the bottom of the CB line, square across to draw a horizontal line the length of the half-neckline measurement. Measure along the horizontal line, and mark the distance of the shoulder point from the CB (the first measurement you took in Step 1). Square up 4″–6″ (10–15 cm) from the shoulder point.

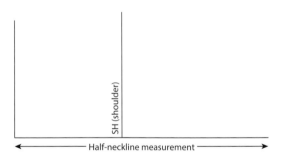

NOTE

The horizontal line is the neckline edge of the collar. The line between the CB and the shoulder point will match to the (half) back neckline of the garment, and the extended line beyond the shoulder will match to the front neckline.

CLASSIC SHIRT COLLAR AND STAND

Skill Level: Intermediate to Confident

This is a classic shirt collar that can be used for men's, women's, and children's clothing. The stand attaches to the neckline and creates a firm base for the fall of the separate collar. The stand on its own can also be used as a mandarin collar.

Develop a Collar and Stand Pattern

1. On the collar draft (previous page), measure and mark ¾ of the half-neckline measurement from the CB out on the horizontal line. Then measure and mark a point above the front end of the horizontal line: ½" (12 mm) above for adults and ¼"–⅜" (6–10 mm) above for children's wear. Draw a line to connect these 2 points, and then use a curved ruler to blend the new angle into a smooth upward curve from close to the shoulder line to the CF. This is the front neckline of the collar stand.

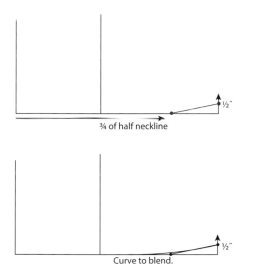

¾ of half neckline

½"

Curve to blend.

½"

2. Measure along the curved line and mark the front neckline measurement on the curve,

extending or shortening the curved line if necessary. Also mark in the position of the CF on the curved line by measuring the button extension width back from the front edge. Square up 1¼" (32 mm) from each of these points.

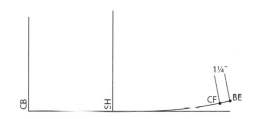

CB   SH   1¼"   CF   BE

3. Choose the height of the collar stand you'd like to make. For children's wear, try about ¾" (2 cm); for an adult's shirt, a minimum of 1" (2.5 cm) is a good standard, although you can make it higher. Measure the collar stand height up from the neckline edge, and draw a parallel line to make the top edge. Draw a curve, from the CF line on the top edge to about ⅔ of the way down the upright outer line of the button extension, to round off the end of the collar stand. This is the collar stand draft.

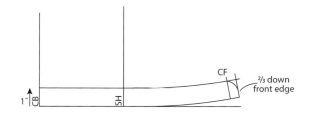

1"   CB   SH   CF   ⅔ down front edge

4. To begin the collar piece, mirror the top line of the collar stand from the CB to the CF (you can fold the paper and trace it).

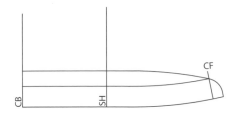

5. Draw in the shape of the collar above the line you just drew. It can be any depth, but for a standard dress shirt you can begin with a horizontal line at least 1½˝ (4 cm) above the line (see Tip, below). Add a cut-on-fold arrow at the CB line on both the collar and stand.

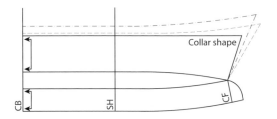

 Take some measurements from an existing shirt collar, or drape muslin around your neck to estimate the depth and shape of the collar. Don't stress too much at this stage, because it can all be adjusted before finalizing the pattern. Collar patterns often need a little tweaking before they are the shape you want them to be.

6. See Trace a Full Pattern from a Half-Draft (page 22) to trace full patterns from the draft, adding ¼˝ (6 mm) seam allowances all the way around both pieces. Notch the CF, CB, and shoulder points on the bottom edge of the stand. Notch the CB and CF on the top edge of the stand and the lower edge of the collar.

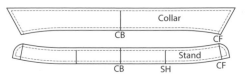

Check and Tweak the Pattern

It's important to make a quick mock-up in muslin to check that the collar has the right shape and fit around the neckline before finalizing your pattern.

1. Fuse interfacing to some muslin and cut out 1 collar and 1 stand. Stitch these together, matching the top edge of the stand to the bottom edge of the collar, and attach them to the neckline of the test garment.

2. Check the shape of the collar and the width and position of the points. If you want the collar to be smaller, draw the shape that you want on the muslin or trim it to size. If you want it wider, you can pin or stitch on some extra muslin and draw on that.

3. Check the fall of the collar piece. The rule of thumb is that the straighter the collar pattern, the more upright (parallel to the neck) the collar will sit. A classic narrow shirt collar is often quite straight, but if you want the collar to sit flatter and further from the neck, you will need to make some adjustments, as follows.

4. Cut into the muslin at regular intervals and pin the collar edge where you would like it to sit. Measure and make a clear note of the spaces that appear between each cut line—they may all be the same or all quite different. If the measurements are all similar, find the average (add them all together and divide by the number of slash lines) and use it for every slash line.

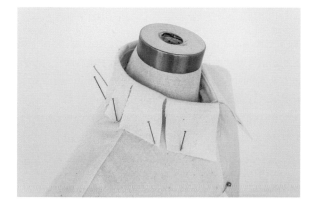

NOTE

If a collar sits too flat and wide, simply reverse this process. Pinch and pin (or slash and overlap) the bottom edge of the collar to make it sit higher around the neck.

5. Trace a copy of the collar draft (remember not to cut the original!), and rule slash lines in

the same positions as the cuts on the muslin collar.

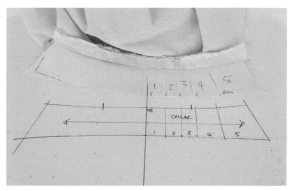

6. Cut the draft along the slash lines. Working on top of another piece of paper, open or close the gaps on the outer edge of the draft to match the measurements on the muslin, keeping the inner edge of the collar joined. Tape the sections of the draft to the paper.

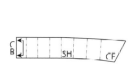
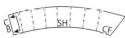

Slash and open.   Slash and close.

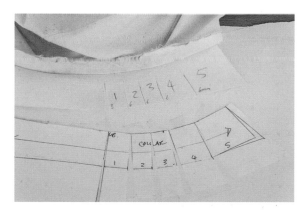

7. Use a French curve to smooth out the lines of the altered draft. Trace a pattern with seam allowances, and make another muslin test collar before cutting your final garment.

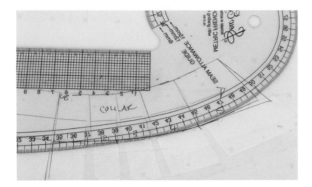

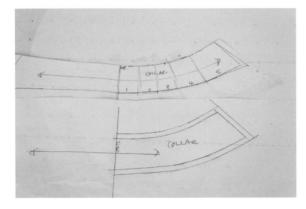

NOTE

You may slash and open without physically cutting the paper. You can trace the pieces in the same manner as you would when closing out a dart (see Waistline Facings for Zippers, page 108).

Trace Patterns for the Collar and Stand

1. When you are happy with the shape of the altered collar, trace a new pattern and add seam allowances all the way around. Mark both the collar and stand patterns with "Cut 2 fabric." Mark the notches at the CF, CB, and shoulder points.

NOTE

Use ¼″ (6 mm) seam allowances on the collar pieces so that you don't have to trim anything as you sew, but remember to make the neck-line seam allowances of the garment the same as those on the bottom edge of the collar stand. These can be ¼″, ⅜″, or ½″ (6 mm, 10 mm, or 12 mm)—whatever makes it easiest for you to sew two curved edges together.

2. Trace a pattern for the collar interfacing, including the seam allowance on the neck edge but without seam allowances for the outer edges. Trace an interfacing pattern for the collar stand that is completely free of seam allowances. Label both "Cut 1 interfacing."

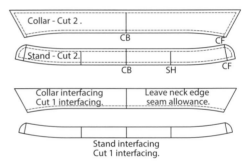

Tip *Optional: To make the collar sit well when it is sewn, make the undercollar slightly smaller than the upper collar. Trace a separate undercollar pattern, or simply trim away a little of the fabric after you have cut the collar piece, gradually reducing the outer edge of the collar by ⅛″ (3 mm). When you sew the collar, gently stretch the undercollar to align the edges with the seam allowances of the upper collar.*

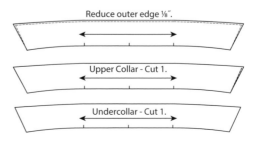

Sew the Collar

1. Cut the fabric and interfacing. Fuse 1 collar and 1 stand with the seam allowances free of interfacing on all but the neck edge of the upper collar (as per the pattern pieces). The collar piece with interfacing is now the upper collar piece, and the other is the underside. The stand with the interfacing is the inner collar stand and the one without is the outer collar stand.

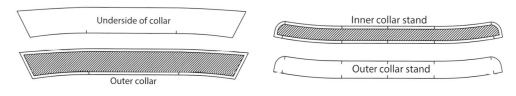

2. With the 2 collar pieces right sides together, backstitch and sew around the outer edges (from one CF corner to the other), pivoting at the corner points. Backstitch neatly, and press the seam to settle the stitches into the fabric.

3. Turn the corner points of the collar. Depending on the weight of your fabric, there are 2 options.

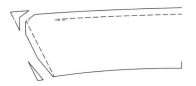

If the Fabric Is Heavyweight

1. Reduce the bulk by snipping the seam allowances at a steep angle from each side of the corner point.

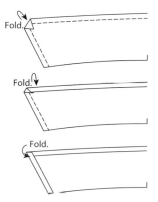

2. Press the seams open or to the underside of the collar. If the upper-collar shape is curved, understitch (page 30) the seam allowances to the underside of the collar.

If the Fabric Is Lightweight

For fabric that is lightweight (for example, lawn or voile) to standard shirting-weight fabric, it's best to preserve the structure of the fabric so the point doesn't weaken and fray. At the pivot point of the stitch line, fold the corner of the seam allowance toward the underside of the collar. Press or finger-press it in place. Fold the outer and side edge seam allowances neatly from the stitch lines in toward the center of the collar underside. Press them in place.

If the Fabric Is Medium-Weight

With medium-weight fabric, I do a halfway measure: I clip the corners of the underside of the collar, as for bulky fabric, and fold the upper-collar seam allowances, as for lightweight fabric.

TURN THE COLLAR

To turn a neat corner, it's important to keep the seam allowances as flat as possible within the point. Poking something into a corner often pushes the seam allowance into a lump. You can buy various types of point-turning gadgets, and you might already have a favorite method. I usually prefer to use my thumb and finger, as follows.

Finger Turning Method

1. Poke your thumb into the corner of the collar, with the top of the thumbnail as tight into the corner as possible.

2. Use your forefinger or middle finger to hold the seam allowances open or pressed to the side (as prepared earlier) as you align the top edge of your fingernail with the point of the collar. Your thumbnail and fingernail should be aligned on either side of the fabric.

3. Holding the thumbnail and fingernail firmly together, flip the collar right side out. Squeeze and shape the corner so that it lies flat and

pointed, with the seam allowances as flat as possible inside. If necessary, use a tailor's awl or large needle to gently ease out the point.

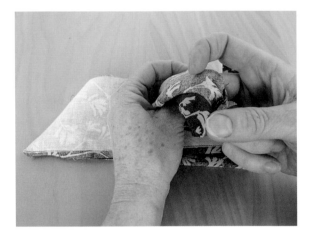

NOTE

For particularly sharp corners, you can use pointy tweezers in the same way as the thumb-and-finger method to hold the seam allowances firmly in place as you flip the fabric over the point.

PRESS AND TOPSTITCH THE COLLAR

1. Press the collar flat, taking care that from the upper side of the collar the underside is not visible around the outer edge. The pressing or understitching you did earlier should make this easy.

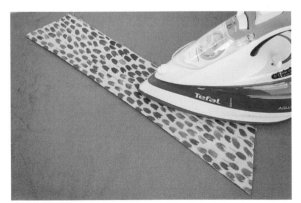

2. Topstitch around the collar between a generous ¹⁄₁₆″ and ¼″ (2 mm and 6 mm) from the seamed edge, pivoting on the corner points and backstitching neatly at each end.

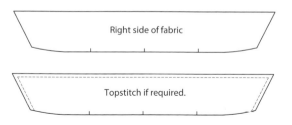

3. *Optional:* Fold the outer edge of the collar toward the underside, and stitch the raw edges of the neck seam allowances together ⅛″ (3 mm) from the raw edge.

Attach the Collar Stand to the Collar

1. On the (interfaced) inner collar stand, press the neckline seam allowance toward the wrong side of the fabric.

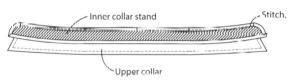

Press.

 You can use the fusible tape turning trick (page 32) here.

2. With right sides together, match the (unturned) top seam allowance of the inner collar stand to the raw edge at the bottom of the upper collar. Align the ends of the collar to the CF notches on the stand, and match the CB notches. Stitch the collar in place slightly narrower than the actual seam allowance.

Inner collar stand — Stitch.

Upper collar

3. Place the outer collar stand on the underside of the collar, right sides together. With the collar sandwiched in the middle, align the raw edges of both collar stands. If you unfold the turned neckline seam allowance, the raw edges of both the inner and outer collar stands should align.

4. With the turning on the inner collar stand unfolded, place a pin at the crease line of the turning at each end, holding the 2 stands together. Using the pin as a guide (so as not to stitch onto the seam allowance), backstitch neatly and then sew all the way around the top edge of the collar stand. Finish with a neat backstitch at the crease-line pin at the other end of the stand.

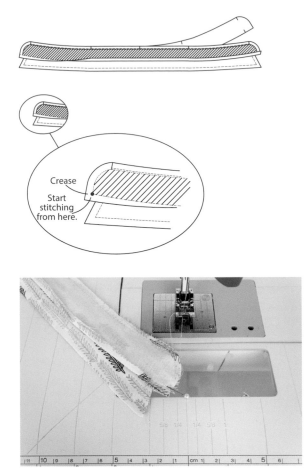

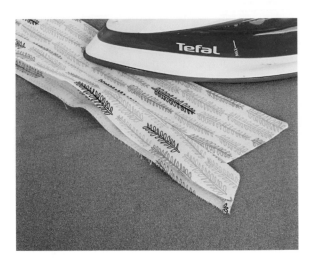

Tip *It is easier to turn through the curved seam allowances at the front of the collar stand if you pink the edges.*

5. If you have used a seam allowance wider than ¼″ (6 mm), trim the seam allowance down to ¼″ (6 mm) now. Turn the collar stand right side out and press it flat, with the turning at the neckline edge folded to the inside.

Attach the Collar to the Garment

1. Construct the garment to the point where the darts, pockets, button plackets/facings, and shoulder seams / yoke are all finished.

2. Match the outer collar stand (without interfacing) to the neckline edge of the garment, right sides together. At the point where you are beginning to sew, align the neckline seam allowances. Check that the edge of the button placket/facing is sitting as close to the seam on the collar stand as it can without overlapping onto the seam allowances. You might need to use an awl or pins to keep it in place as you begin to sew. Backstitch neatly, level with the folded edge of the turning on the inner collar stand.

3. Matching the notches on the shoulder, CB, and CF, carefully align the raw edges and stitch the collar stand to the garment, keeping a very even, accurate seam allowance. Take care to match the other end of the collar stand to the edge of the button placket/facing on the other side of the garment.

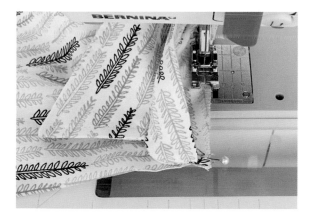

Sewing without Pins

1. *Once you have placed the needle through the stitch line at the CF, reach ahead to the shoulder notch on the undercollar and match it to the shoulder seam, holding the layers together between your right thumb and forefinger.*

2. *Move your right hand in front of the needle to straighten the neckline slightly (but don't stretch the fabric). With the fingers of your left hand holding the fabric along the seamline in front of the needle, align the raw edges of the seam allowances between the CF and the shoulder notch. Use whatever spare fingers you have on your right hand to help align and hold the fabric as you sew with an accurate seam allowance.*

3. *Repeat this action between each set of notches—shoulder to CB, CB to shoulder, and shoulder to CF—and onto the button extension.*

Finish the Collar

As with every aspect of garment construction, there are several ways to attach a collar. The top-stitch method is the standard mass-production method. The burrito method is a more handcrafted shirt-making technique, which I prefer to use because it makes it easier to achieve a neater finish at the front of the collar stand, where it is most obvious.

TOP-STITCH METHOD

1. Turn the collar stand up and press the neckline seam allowances into it. Keep the turnings in the CF ends of the collar stand as flat as possible and tucked behind the neckline seam allowances of the shirt placket. This keeps the bulk of the raw edges out of the way.

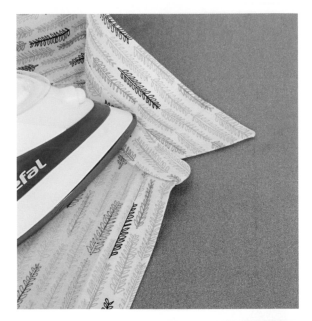

2. Align the folded edge of the turning on the inner collar stand to just cover the neckline seam, and press it in place. Use pins or fusible tape to hold it. Edgestitch all around the collar stand, catching the inner collar in place a generous 1⁄16″ (2 mm) from the folded edge of the turning.

BURRITO METHOD

The burrito method allows you to "bag out" the front of the collar to enclose the raw edges. You need to turn the very ends of the collar stand inside out and stitch the neckline of the garment between the two collar stand pieces.

1. Turn the collar stand wrong side out. Roll or push the point of the collar and the front of the garment back into the stand so that for about 1″ (2.5 cm) you can align the neckline seam allowances of both inner and outer collar stands. Pin it in place.

2. Stitch along the original neckline seam to attach the inner collar stand for as far as you can comfortably align the seam allowances. Depending on the width of the collar stand, this might be as little as ¾″ (2 cm) or up to 4″ (10 cm).

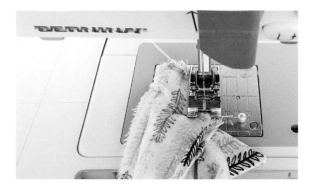

3. Pull the collar out and turn the stand right side out, taking care to smooth out the curved

edges at each end. Tuck the remaining (turned) neckline seam allowance into the collar stand, and press.

4. Use a tailor's awl or fusible tape to hold the folded edge of the turned seam allowance in place over the neckline seam, and edgestitch it in place. Edgestitch all the way around the entire collar stand.

5. Continue to make the garment and add buttons and buttonholes (see Marking and Sewing Buttons, page 68). The buttonhole on a collar stand is always horizontal, beginning at the CF and extending toward the back of the garment, while the buttonholes on the shirt front are always vertical and centered on the pattern.

CONVERTIBLE COLLAR

Skill Level: Basic to Intermediate

A convertible collar is a relaxed style that is most commonly used on casual shirts for men, women, and children. It can also be used on dresses, pajamas, and casual jackets. It is usually worn open, but it can button up to the neckline.

Prepare the Facing Pattern

1. Follow the steps for preparing the garment draft (page 21). On the garment front draft, add a button extension (page 58) at the CF if one does not already exist. Trace the garment pattern from the draft, and make a muslin test garment.

NOTE

For a shirt with a yoke, you can make the neckline seam allowances ¼″ (6 mm); otherwise, use ½″ (12 mm) seam allowances.

2. On the draft, draw in a facing that follows the shape of the neckline and runs parallel to the edge of the button extension. The facing needs to be at least 2″ (5 cm) wide but can be wider if large buttons are to be used or if the shirt is a style that might be worn open. For large garments (for example, men's shirts), use at least 3″ (7.5 cm) facings. Blend the area between the neckline and the button extension with a smooth curve.

3. Trace a pattern for the facing. Add seam allowances to match those on the garment pattern, notching the CF on the neckline edge. No seam allowances are necessary on the inner edge of the facing.

NOTE

You may prefer to make a folded facing by tracing the facing onto the front garment piece, mirrored along the button extension line.

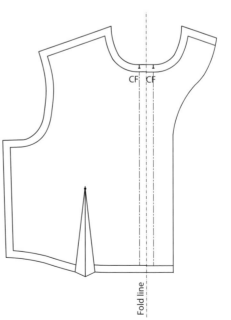

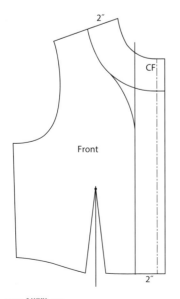

Prepare the Collar Pattern

1. Follow Prepare the Collar Draft, Steps 1 and 2 (page 124).

2. Measure ¼" (6 mm) up from the front end of the neckline and mark a dot.

3. From the CB on the neckline edge of the collar draft, measure ¾ of the half-neckline measurement. Mark this position with a dot, and then connect the 2 dots with a line.

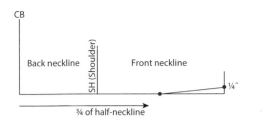

4. Using a curved ruler edge, smooth the corner off at the ¾ mark to make a gentle upward curve on the neckline of the draft. Measure from the shoulder toward the front of the draft, and mark the front neckline measurement on the new line.

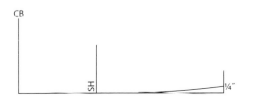

5. On the CB line, measure the width of the desired collar plus ¾" (2 cm) up from the neckline; for wide collars, add more. Square across from the collar width measurement on the CB line to make the outer edge of the collar. Draw in an estimation of the collar point shape.

Don't agonize over this measurement. You will be able to tweak the collar shape later, or you can copy the shape of the collar on a favorite shirt.

6. Trace a pattern for the collar, with the CB line on the fold of the paper so that you can cut a full pattern. For a shirt with a yoke, add ¼" (6 mm) seam allowances all the way around the collar. For a shirt with no yoke, add ½" (12 mm) seam allowances at the neckline and ¼" (6 mm) around the outer edges of the collar. Notch the CB, shoulder, and CF.

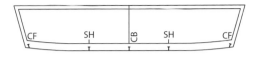

Check and Tweak the Pattern

1. Cut 1 collar piece from muslin and 1 from interfacing, and fuse the interfacing into place. Using the largest stitch on your sewing machine, sew the collar to the neckline of the muslin test garment.

2. Check the shape of the collar on a dress form or person. Mark the collar muslin, or make notes on adjustments that you would like to make to the width or shape of the collar. If the collar is sitting too high or too flat, make adjustments with slash and open/close lines (see Classic Shirt Collar and Stand, Check and Tweak the Pattern, page 126).

3. Adjust the collar draft as necessary, and trace a new pattern. Cut the revised pattern from interfaced muslin, and check the fit and shape. Adjust as necessary until you are happy to proceed to the final garment.

Sew the Collar

1. Cut the garment pieces, including interfacing for both of the front facing pieces. Fuse the interfacing, and finish the inner (curved) edge of the facing. For a garment with no yoke, also serge the shoulder seam allowance.

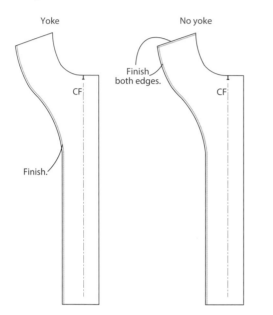

2. Cut 2 collar pieces from fabric and 1 piece from interfacing. Remove the outer seam allowances on the interfacing to reduce bulk, but leave the neckline seam allowance. Fuse the interfacing to the upper collar piece, and trim ⅛″ (3 mm) from the outer edge of the undercollar piece.

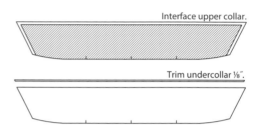

3. Follow the process for sewing the collar (see Classic Shirt Collar and Stand, page 125), turning it through and topstitching as required.

Attach the Collar

You can use these same methods for convertible collars and Peter Pan collars with facings (see Collars, page 122).

A Shirt with No Yoke *Skill Level: Basic to Intermediate*

1. Construct the garment to the point where the darts, pockets, button plackets/facings are all finished. Sew the shoulder seams of the garment and serge them closed (or use another seam finish, page 28).

2. With the underside of the collar against the right side of the garment, match the collar neckline to the neckline of the garment. Find the point where the ½″ (12 mm) seam allowance depth crosses the sewn edge at the front of the collar, and then place that point level with the CF notch on the garment.

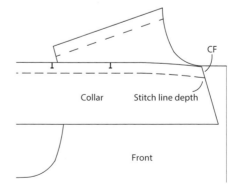

3. Lift the upper collar out of the way so that you can sew the underside piece to the garment. With the raw edges of the seam allowances flush, backstitch at the seam allowance depth about ½″ (12 mm) from the end of the collar.

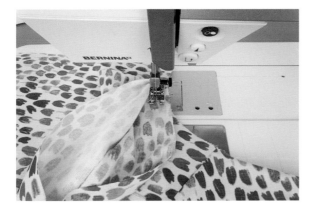

4. Matching the notches on the collar to the notches and seams on the garment, sew the collar in place, taking care to keep the seam allowances accurate (see Sewing without Pins, page 133).

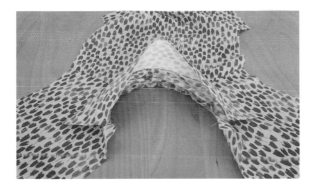

5. On the garment fronts, align the raw edges of the upper collar with those of the neckline and undercollar. Stitch the collar in place (on the garment front only) between the CF edges and about 1″ (2.5 cm) from the shoulder seam.

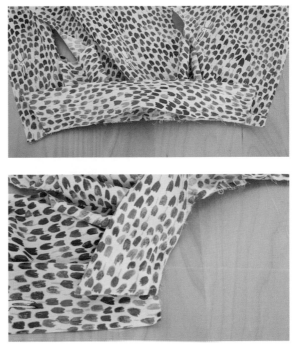

6. With the right sides of the fabric together, align the facing along the button extension edges of the garment and stitch it in place, backstitching at both ends of the seam. Clip the corners of the seam allowances at both ends, and press the seam open. Fold the facing back into place on the right side of the garment, keeping the seam allowances pressed open.

NOTE

If it is a folded facing, simply fold it into place on the right side of the garment.

7. Align and pin together all the layers of the facing, collar, and garment at the neckline edge. With a ½″ (12 mm) seam allowance, backstitch on the corner of the button extension. Take care to match the shoulder seam allowances of the garment and facing, and stitch all the layers together to about ¾″ (2 cm) from the shoulder seam. Backstitch securely.

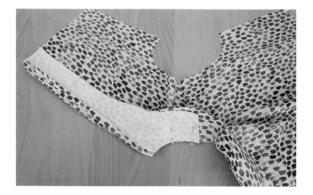

8. Snip the seam allowances at a 45° angle—from the CF side toward the last stitch of the seam—on each side of the collar. Snip into the curve of the neckline seam allowances every ¼″–⅜″ (6–10 mm). On smaller garments, trim the seam allowance of this curve to ¼″ (6 mm).

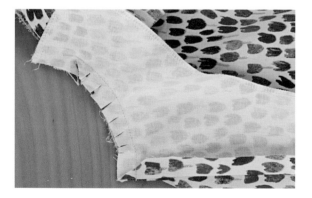

9. Turn the facings to the right side and flip the remaining facing, collar, and garment neckline seam allowances up into the collar, keeping them all flat. Turn and press the seam allowance of the upper collar under, and carefully press it in place to overlap the neckline seam by 1⁄16″ (1.5 mm).

10. Use fusible tape, pins, or a tailor's awl to hold the neckline turning as you edgestitch it securely in place, backstitching neatly at both ends.

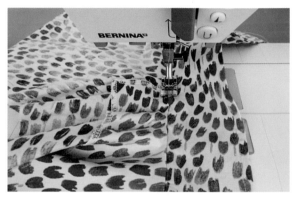

11. Secure the outer edge of the facing to the garment at the shoulder seam with a discreet backstitch on the seam allowances.

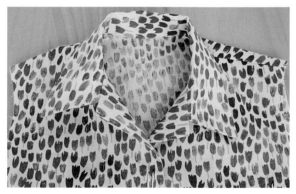

NOTE

If you're altering a dress pattern, see Attaching a Skirt with a Folded Button Facing (page 113).

A Shirt with a Yoke *Skill Level: Intermediate*

1. Construct the garment to the point where any darts and pockets are finished. With right sides together, sew the bottom edge of the outer yoke to the shirt back, backstitching at both ends of the seam. In the same manner, attach the shirt front pieces to the outer yoke at the shoulders.

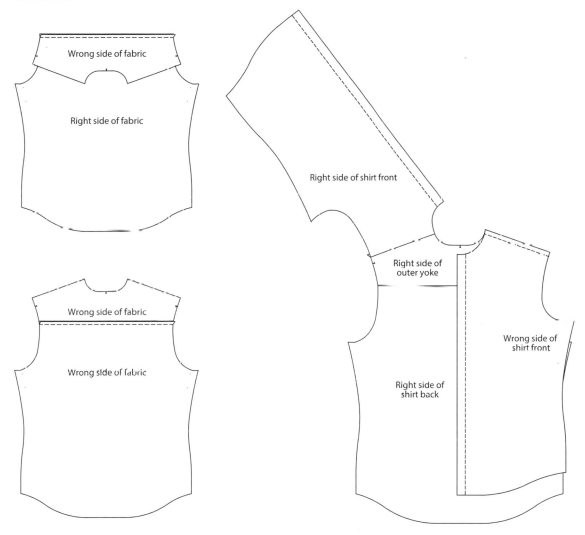

2. Match the facings to the inner yoke, aligning each at the neckline end of the shoulder seams, with right sides together. Stitch each facing in place on the yoke with a ½″ (12 mm) seam allowance, backstitching at

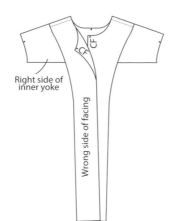

Right side of inner yoke

Wrong side of facing

CF

CF

both ends of each seam. If your garment has a folded facing, this means the yoke will be attached to the garment front as well.

3. On both outer and inner yoke pieces, press all the shoulder seam allowances toward the yoke, including the shoulder edges of the inner yoke that are not attached to the facing. Clip the corners of the seam allowances at the neckline edge of the shoulder seams to reduce bulk.

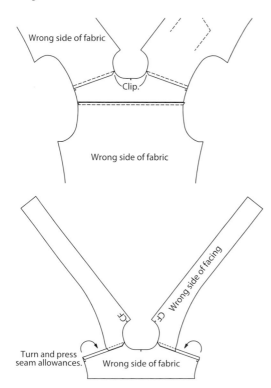

Wrong side of fabric

Clip.

Wrong side of fabric

Wrong side of facing

CF

CF

Turn and press seam allowances.

Wrong side of fabric

4. With right sides together, match the under-collar neckline to the neckline of the garment. Find the point where the seam allowance depth of the collar crosses the sewn edge at the front of the collar, and then place that point level with the CF notch.

Attaching a collar to a shirt with folded facings

5. Take care to keep all the seam allowances flush along the raw edges. Sew the collar in place through all the layers of fabric, matching the notches on the collar to the seams and notches on the garment.

6. Match the facings and yoke to the garment, right sides together, with the collar sandwiched between. If you're using "grown on" folded facings, simply fold them into place. If you're using a separate facing, stitch the facing to the shirt along the button extension edge at the required seam allowance depth, backstitching at both ends of the seam. Clip the corners of the seam allowances and press them open.

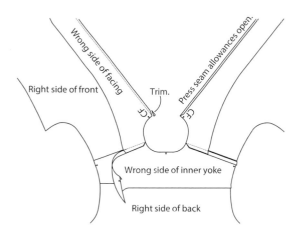

7. Match the raw neckline edges of the inner yoke and facing to those on the outer yoke and collar. Stitch them together, keeping the notches aligned and the seam allowance accurate.

8. Snip into the neckline seam allowance every ⅜″ (1 cm), taking care not to snip the stitches. Clip the corners if necessary to reduce bulk.

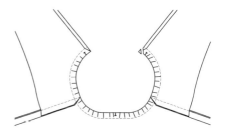

9. Turn the garment right side out, and press the facings flat to the inside.

10. Align the shoulder seams of the inner and outer yokes. Flip the bottom edge of the inner yoke piece up, and at the shoulder point pinch the seam allowances of the inner and outer yoke together.

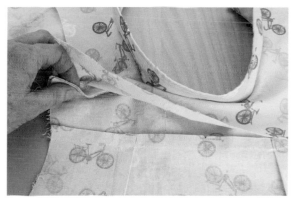

Holding the seam allowances together in this position (with the shirt front sandwiched in between), backstitch and sew the yoke shoulder seams together from the outer edge toward the neckline. It is important to sew with an accurate seam allowance and not stretch or ease the inner yoke. Stop and backstitch when it becomes too difficult to see where you are sewing. Repeat for the other shoulder seam.

11. Sewing the bottom edge of the inner and outer yokes together requires that the shirt front, back, and collar be between the 2 yoke pieces. Roll each piece up and onto the yoke, and then fold the inner yoke over the top. Align the bottom edges of the yoke pieces, with the back shirt piece sandwiched in between, and stitch them together, following the original seamline and backstitching at both ends of the seam. Use a zipper foot if necessary, and take extra care not to catch any of the rolled-up garment in the seam.

12. Pull all the shirt pieces out of the yoke sandwich, and press the yoke flat.

PETER PAN COLLAR
Skill Level: Basic to Intermediate

A Peter Pan collar is a relatively flat collar that is always worn closed. It frames the neckline with either a single piece (opening only at the front) or two pieces (opening at the CF and CB) and is commonly used on blouses, dresses, and children's wear with either CF or CB zippers or button closures.

This collar can be completely flat against the garment or have a roll (stand) height of up to 1" (2.5 cm) at the CB. A flat Peter Pan collar can be as wide as you want it to be and any shape (including a sailor collar), and it can be added to a neckline of almost any depth or shape. I use Helen Joseph-Armstrong's method (see Further Reading, page 174), which builds in the height of the roll as it is drafted and requires very little tweaking.

Flat roll

Low roll

High roll

Begin with a pattern that has the neckline that you want to use, or alter a pattern to create a new neckline shape and facings (see Necklines, page 71).

NOTE

On a Peter Pan collar with either a button or zippered closure, neckline facings may be used. For a simple finish, you may also choose to make a folded button facing (page 59) and finish the neckline with binding (page 149).

Develop the Collar Pattern

1. Trace a draft of the front bodice, leaving enough space on the paper to trace the back draft (joining the front to the back at the shoulder seams), but don't trace the back just yet.

2. Prepare to trace the back draft, joining the shoulder seamlines and matching the neckline edges. Depending how high you want to make the stand of the collar, you will overlap the shoulder points by anywhere between ½″ (12 mm) for a flat collar and 4″ (10 cm) for a high collar.

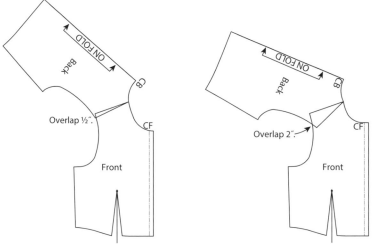

Flat roll   Low roll   High roll

3. Rule a line to extend the CB line ⅛″ (3 mm) above the neckline, and then square across about 1″ (2–3 cm).

4. For a medium- or high-roll collar, measure ⅜″–½″ (10–12 mm) down from the neckline at the CF. For a low or flat collar, measure ¼″ (6 mm). Draw the collar neckline in a smooth curve from this new mark on the CF to the line above the CB, staying as close to the original neckline and shoulder point as possible.

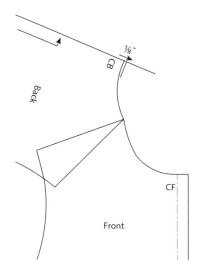

5. Measure the original neckline on the garment draft between the shoulder and the CB and then from the shoulder to the CF. To make the collar fit to the garment, measure the collar line out from either side of the shoulder point (toward the CF and CB), and mark the corresponding garment neckline measurements with a new CF and CB. This is called *trueing the neckline measurement*.

6. Square down from the CB mark on the collar neckline. Estimate the width and shape of the collar (or use another garment as a guide), and draw it over the garment draft between the new collar CF and CB.

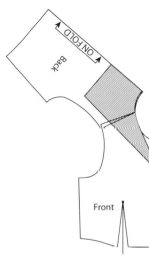

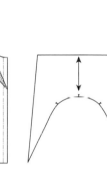

Sailor collar

Pointed collar

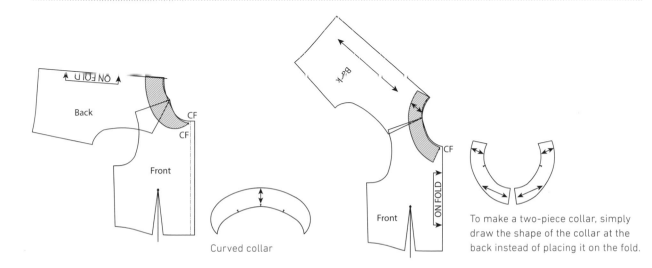

Curved collar

To make a two-piece collar, simply draw the shape of the collar at the back instead of placing it on the fold.

7. Mark the CB of the collar with "Cut on fold" (unless you're making a two-piece collar). Make a full pattern from the half-draft of the collar (see Trace a Full Pattern from a Half-Draft, page 22), and then make a muslin test of the collar. (The straight grain is parallel to the CB.) Slash and open/close (page 125) to tweak the fit and shape before making a final pattern.

8. Trace a final pattern with your preferred seam allowances.

Cut and Sew the Collar

1. Cut an upper collar and undercollar from fabric. Cut an upper collar from interfacing—remove the outer-edge seam allowances to reduce bulk. Fuse the interfacing to the wrong side of the upper collar piece. Reduce the outer edge of the undercollar by ⅛″ (3 mm).

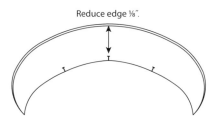

Reduce edge ⅛″.

2. With the right sides of the fabric together, stitch the collar pieces together around the outer seamline, stretching the undercollar slightly to align the edges of the seam allowances.

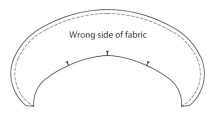

Wrong side of fabric

Tip Sew with the undercollar on top on the sewing machine so that the upper collar is gently eased onto it (see Easing, page 29).

3. Understitch (page 30) the seam allowances to the undercollar; then trim or pink the seam allowance edges to ⅛″ (3 mm).

NOTE

Understitch only on the areas of the seam that you can see and keep flat. Don't attempt to begin or finish too far into a corner or tight curve, or you will stitch puckers in the fabric.

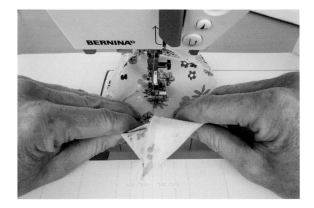

4. Turn the collar through to the right side and press it flat, aligning the neckline seam allowances of the upper collar and undercollar. Topstitch the outer edge of the collar.

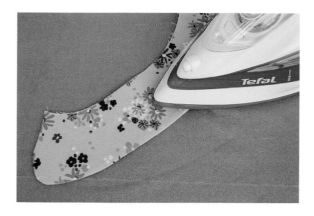

Attach the Collar

FRONT BUTTON AND NECKLINE FACING

Skill Level: Basic to Intermediate

This is suitable for medium- or high-roll Peter Pan collars. Follow the directions for a convertible collar (page 136) to sew the collar and front facing to the garment.

BOUND NECKLINE SEAMS

Skill Level: Basic

This method works well for garments with a folded button facing (page 59) and a collar with a medium roll. It's a quick method for simple garments and a good solution when using sheer fabrics that would allow a full facing to show through.

1. Construct the garment to the point where the shoulder seams are joined, the seam allowances are finished, and the inside edges of the button facing edges are finished.

2. Staystitch the neckline edge of the collar and garment.

Tip On a high-roll collar, turn under the areas where the roll will be highest as you sew along the neckline. This will make the collar sit in a curve on the garment.

3. Place the collar right side up on the right side of the garment, aligning the neckline seam allowances. Match the CF, CB, and shoulder notches of the collar to the garment as you stitch it in place.

4. With right sides together, fold the facings into place at the opening of the garment. Aligning the CF notches, stitch across the neckline edge of each facing to join it to the garment and collar.

7. Cut small snips into the most curved areas of the neckline seam allowances without cutting the seam; then fold and press the binding around to the underside of the seam, covering all the raw edges. Use fusible tape to help hold it in place.

5. Make bias binding using a ¾″ (18 mm) bias tape maker (page 15), or use purchased ¾″ (18 mm) bias binding. Cut a piece to generously fit the length of the neckline.

6. With the collar facing upward, place the bias binding right side down on the neckline seam, with the end of the binding about ¼″ (6 mm) in from the corner of the facing. Open up the folded turning of the binding and align the raw edges with those of the neckline seam allowances. Stitch along the crease, gently curving (but not stretching) the binding. Finish stitching ¼″ (6 mm) from the other end of the neckline seam, and trim off the excess binding.

8. Turn the button facings right side out, taking care to pull the corner points through. Press the binding downward, using steam as you gently curve it and flatten it against the garment.

9. Beginning on the edge of the facing, just before the point where the binding emerges, backstitch and stitch a generous 1/16″ (2 mm) from the folded edge to attach the bottom edge of the bound seam allowances to the garment. Finish on the beginning of the facing on the other side, and backstitch neatly.

FULL NECKLINE FACING

Skill Level: Basic to Intermediate

A flat Peter Pan collar sits best with a full neckline facing (page 71) with a zipper or buttons.

1. Construct the garment to the point where the shoulder seams are joined and the seam allowances are finished. Staystitch the neckline edge.

2. Staystitch the neckline edges of the collar together.

3. Place the collar right side up on the right side of the garment, aligning the neckline seam

allowances. Match the CF, CB, and shoulder notches of the collar to the garment as you stitch it in place.

4. Follow the directions for drafting and sewing a full neckline facing (see Neckline Facings, page 71). The collar is sandwiched between the garment and facing when you sew.

Cuffs, Plackets, and Sleeves

A short-sleeve shirt can become a long-sleeve shirt if you know how to draft and sew a cuff and placket.

A cuff adds definition to the end of the sleeve. It narrows the shape of the sleeve toward the wrist by holding pleats or gathers and has an overlapped button closure. To allow the hand to pass through, the sleeve opens with a bound placket just above the cuff. I have included two types of plackets here: a classic shirt-sleeve placket (page 157) and a "hidden" continuous bound placket (page 162) for more minimalist designs.

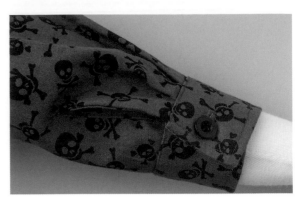

Classic shirt-sleeve placket

Continuous bound placket

CUFF DRAFT

Skill Level: Basic

A simple shirt cuff can be anywhere between 1″ and 3″ (2.5 cm and 7.5 cm) wide (also called *cuff depth*). It needs to create structure at the end of the sleeve but be loose enough to accommodate arm movement.

Make a Cuff Pattern

1. If you don't have a garment to use as a guide for the cuff circumference, measure around the hand of the person who will wear the shirt—mid-palm and not including the thumb—and add ½″ (12 mm) to this measurement. Use this as a starting point, and also decide on the cuff depth you'd like.

2. Draft a rectangle that is double (2 times) the depth of the desired cuff by the length of the cuff circumference. On one of the short ends, add an extra ¾″ (2 cm) for a button extension.

3. Add a seam allowance all the way around the cuff pattern, fold it in half lengthwise, and notch the midway points on both short ends. Rule a grainline parallel to the fold line. Trace a pattern for the interfacing from the draft with no seam allowance. For less stiffness in the cuff, trace the pattern to half the width of the cuff draft (that is, the actual cuff depth).

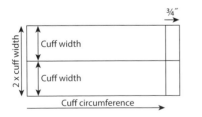

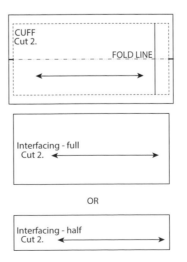

Prepare the Sleeve Pattern

1. Trace a draft copy of the sleeve pattern with a straight grainline through the center. Square across from the central grainline to connect the top corners of the seamlines with a straight line. This is the bicep line.

2. Lengthen the sleeve as desired, measuring the length from the highest point in the center of the sleeve. Square across in both directions from the grainline to make the wrist line. Extend the underarm seamlines at the sides of the sleeve to the wrist line. Fold the sleeve along the central grainline to check that the seamlines are the same shape on both sides. Make a muslin test garment to check the fit of the sleeve before developing it further.

NOTE

Keep the seamlines straight for a full sleeve. For a fitted sleeve, curve them inward.

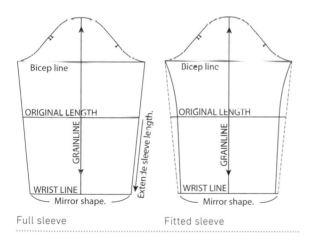

Full sleeve   Fitted sleeve

3. Measure the cuff depth back from the wrist line (subtracting from the sleeve length, not adding to it), and square across the width of the sleeve at this point.

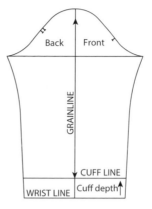

4. On the wrist line, measure and mark the halfway point between the center grainline and the seam on the back side of the sleeve. Square up from this point 2″–3″ (4–7.5 cm)—smaller for children's wear, larger for adults—to make the placket slit.

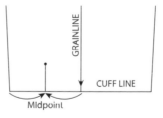

5. *Optional:* To allow for extra fabric for a bending elbow, measure ¼″ (6 mm) for children's wear to ½″ (12 mm) for adults below the cuff line and extend the placket slit line to this point. Using a curved ruler, rule a smooth curve to connect the seamlines to the extended placket line.

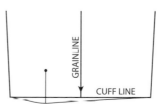

6. For a classic sleeve placket (next page), measure the length of the curved cuff line and then subtract the measurement of the wrist circumference on the cuff pattern. The excess will be the pleat measurement. For a continuous bound placket (page 162), subtract ½" (12 mm) from this excess measurement. To make 2 pleats, divide the measurement in half. If the excess makes pleats of more than 1¼" (3 cm), you may consider narrowing the width of the sleeve.

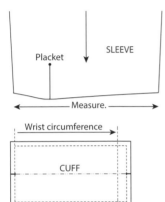

NOTE

Alternatively, a sleeve may be gathered to the cuff for a classic feminine look. You do not need to mark pleats, but you will need to test and tweak the fullness in the sleeve before cutting the final garment.

7. Measuring along the cuff line toward the center of the sleeve, mark the first pleat notch ¾" (2 cm) from the placket slit for children's wear or 1" (2.5 cm) for adults. Measure from this notch and mark the pleat width with another notch. If there is a second pleat, measure another ½"–¾" (1.2–2 cm) from the end of the first pleat before notching the second pleat position.

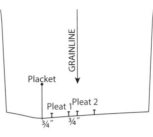

8. Trace a pattern, adding seam allowances and transferring all notches to the outer edge. Add labels, cutting instructions ("Cut 2" or "Cut 1 pair"), and the grainline. Make a test garment to check that the sleeve is the correct shape and length. Tweak the length, width, and fullness, if necessary.

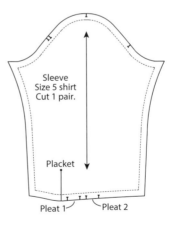

TWO-PIECE CLASSIC SHIRT PLACKET

Skill Level: Intermediate

This classic two-piece placket is the most commonly used method in mass-produced shirts. It has a binding on the underlap and a placket that extends with a top-stitched (reinforcing and decorative) "tower" above the sleeve opening.

Prepare the Placket Pattern

1. Measure the length of the placket slit. Add ½″ (12 mm) to this measurement and draw a rectangle this length by 1½″ (3.5 cm) wide. This is the placket binding pattern.

2. For the outer placket, rule a line that is the length of the placket slit plus the length of the "tower"—anything from 1″ to 4″ (2.5 cm to 10 cm). Square across the top and bottom, and make it into a rectangle that is 2″ (5 cm) wide for children's wear or 2½″ (6.5 cm) wide for adults. Square across to divide the tower from the pocket slit length.

Outer Placket

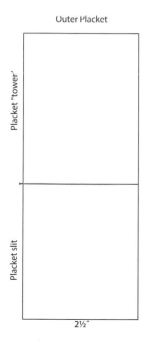

3. Draw a line to divide the rectangle in half lengthwise. In the quarter at the top left of the rectangle, rule a line ½″ (12 mm) above the placket slit line and rule a ¼″ (6 mm) seam allowance to the left of the lengthwise centerline.

Outer Placket

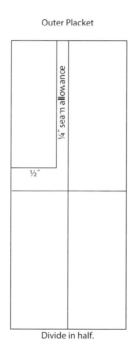

Divide in half.

NOTE

If you're less confident of your sewing skills, you can add a ½″ (12 mm) seam allowance on the vertical edge. It will give you a larger margin to accommodate error.

4. Rule ¼″ (6 mm) seam allowances inside the 2 outer vertical edges of the placket. Cut out the pattern, trimming away the excess in the top left corner.

Outer Placket

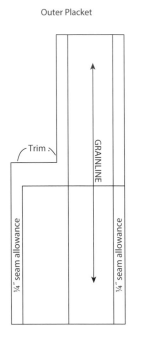

Cut and Sew the Placket

1. Cut 1 pair of sleeves. Mark the placket opening lines on the wrong side of the fabric with a fabric marker, but do not cut them. Cut 1 pair each of outer placket and placket binding pieces.

2. Place a placket binding right side down on the wrong side of each sleeve, on the "back" (or narrower) side of the placket opening line. Align a long edge with the line.

3. Place the outer placket piece right side down, with the shorter edge matching to the binding on the placket opening line. Place a pin ½″ (12 mm) from the top of the placket binding across both pieces to indicate where to stop stitching.

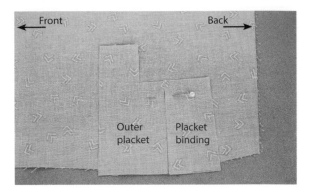

> *Tip* Center and fuse ¼″ (6 mm) fusible tape over the placket opening line, matching the bottom of the tape to the notch on the cuff line of the sleeve and stopping ¼″ (6 mm) below the end of the placket opening. Fuse the placket pieces to hold them securely in place.

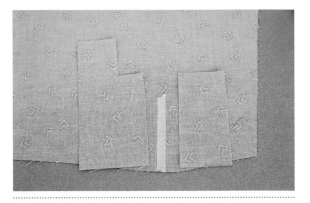

4. Stitch both plackets with a ¼″ (6 mm) seam allowance along the placket opening line, from the bottom edge to ½″ (12 mm) from the top edge. It's important to be accurate here.

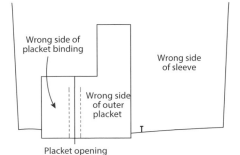

Wrong side of placket binding

Wrong side of sleeve

Wrong side of outer placket

Placket opening

5. Cut along the placket opening line, stopping ¾" (2 cm) from the top edge of the binding and placket. Taking care not to cut the stitches or the seam allowances of the placket pieces, snip the fabric of the *sleeve only* from the placket line toward the top of each line of stitching, forming a V shape with the snips.

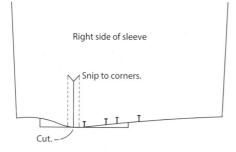

6. Turn the V shape through the opening to the right side of the fabric. Fold it upward from the top of the stitch lines on the plackets, and use a fabric glue stick to hold it firmly in place.

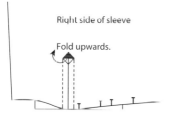

7. Turn each placket piece to the right side, pressing the seam allowances toward the placket opening. Turn the placket pieces through to the right side of the sleeve.

8. Press a ¼" (6 mm) turning along the unattached edge of each placket binding using the fusible tape turning trick (page 32).

9. Place the folded edge of the turning a generous 1/16" (2 mm) over the stitch line on the other side of the binding and fuse it in place, encasing the raw edges. Stitch a generous 1/16" (2 mm) from the turned edge along the full length of the binding.

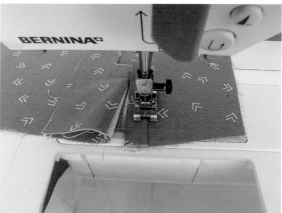

10. Fuse ¼″ (6 mm) fusible tape along the long outer edge of each outer placket piece. Use the backing paper as a folding edge to press a neat turning. Leave the backing paper on.

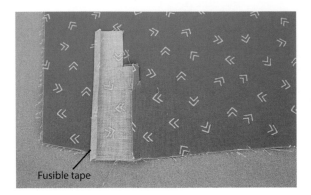

Fusible tape

11. Place the turning over the stitch line, enclosing the raw edges of the seam allowance. Press a crease the length of the folded opening edge, blending it into a turning at the inner edge of the tower.

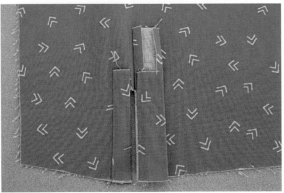

12. Fold a 45° angle from one corner of each placket tower, pressing to make a crease. Fold the remaining point, and press it to make a triangular shape at the top of the tower. Trim away the bulk of the excess fabric on the underside, leaving a ¼″ (6 mm) seam allowance all the way around the tower, and press the tower back into position.

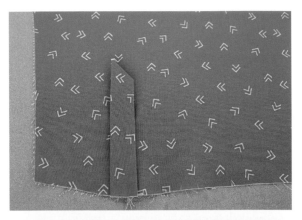

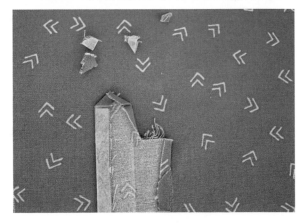

13. Fold the tower down, level with where the placket separates from the binding, and press a crease across it. Rule another line with a Hera marker ¼″ (6 mm) above the crease.

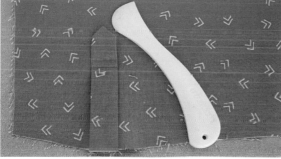

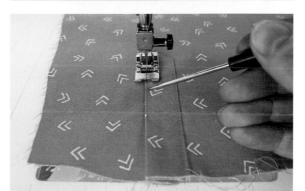

14. Remove the backing paper and fuse the outer placket in place. Use a fabric glue stick to hold the tower in place above the placket, tucking in any raw edges of fabric.

15. Taking care to keep the binding side of the placket opening out of the way, edgestitch a generous ¹⁄₁₆″ (2 mm) from the turned edge of the outer placket. Overlap the placket and binding again, and continue to edgestitch around the top of the tower to the crease line. Pivot and stitch a rectangle-shaped reinforcement, following the Hera marker line. Backstitch securely.

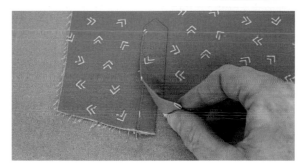

16. Match the notches of each pleat and fold the pick-up away from the placket. Staystitch to hold the pleats in place. Attach the sleeve to the garment; then attach the cuff (page 165).

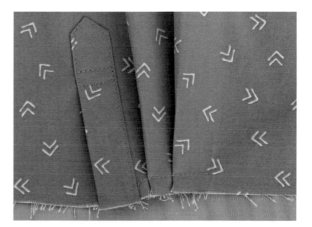

CONTINUOUS BOUND PLACKET
Skill Level: Basic to Intermediate

This is a simple finish for a placket that does not show on the outside of the sleeve. It is a good choice for blouses or shirts where minimal design features are required.

1. Cut the placket slit on the sleeve. For the placket, cut a strip of fabric 1″–1½″ (2.5–4 cm) wide and about 1″ longer than 2 times the length of the placket slit, with the straight grain of the fabric along the length.

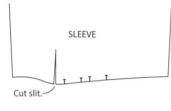

SLEEVE

Cut slit.

1″ | Placket
2 × slit length + 1

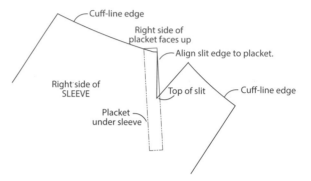

Cuff-line edge

Right side of placket faces up

Align slit edge to placket.

Right side of SLEEVE

Top of slit

Cuff-line edge

Placket under sleeve

2. With the right side of the placket to the wrong side of the sleeve fabric, match the edge of the split with the long edge of the placket strip. Place the pieces under the machine needle with a ¼″ (6 mm) seam allowance. Lower the needle at this point, and lift the presser foot. Realign the sleeve fabric so that the top of the slit (the part furthest from the needle) is sitting a scant ¼″ (5 mm) from the edge of the placket.

3. Stitch, keeping an even ¼″ (6 mm) seam allowance from the edge of the placket, until the needle is sitting level with the end of the slit—a whisker's distance from it. Put the needle down.

4. Raise the presser foot, and pull the sleeve slit open to match the unattached end with the placket edge, mirroring the angle of the sewn side of the slit. The placket strip will stay straight and flat, but the sleeve will buckle up around the top of the slit.

Placket

Sleeve

Placket slit

Continue to stitch with a ¼″ (6 mm) seam allowance to the end of the slit. The sleeve fabric makes a V shape, but the placket seam allowance is an even ¼″ (6 mm).

Right side of placket

Right side of sleeve

Cuff-line edge

¼″ seam allowance

Top of slit

Cuff-line edge

5. Press the seam allowances toward the placket, and then fold a ¼″ (6 mm) turning along the other edge of the placket.

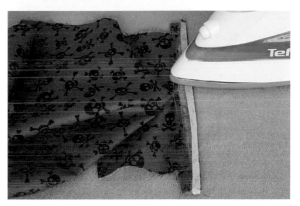

 Use the fusible tape turning trick (page 32).

6. Fold the placket so the folded edge of the turning sits a generous ¹⁄₁₆″ (2 mm) over the stitch line, and press or fuse it in place.

Cuffs, Plackets, and Sleeves 163

7. From the right side of the sleeve, topstitch the placket a generous 1/16″ (2 mm) inside the folded edge of the turning. Take care not to stitch a pucker at the top of the sleeve slit.

8. On the side of the slit that will be toward the front of the garment (the wider side), fold the placket to the wrong side of the sleeve and baste in place within the seam allowance.

9. Fold the placket in half at the top of the slit so the sleeve is right sides together, and backstitch securely through all the layers at an angle to hold the fold together.

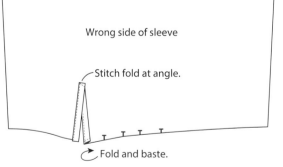

Wrong side of sleeve

Stitch fold at angle.

Fold and baste.

10. Attach the sleeve to the garment, and then attach the cuff (page 165).

SEW THE CUFF

NOTE

The underarm seam of the sleeve must be sewn and finished before the cuff is attached. If you are going to gather the sleeve to the cuff (rather than pleat it), also run a gathering stitch around the cuff-line edge of the sleeve.

1. Cut 2 cuffs and 2 interfacing pieces using the patterns. Fuse the interfacing to the wrong side of the fabric, aligning the edges with the seam allowance depth.

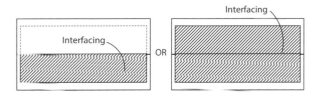

2. Along one long side of each cuff, use the edge of the interfacing as a fold line to turn the seam allowance toward the wrong side of the fabric. Press to crease along the seamline. The half of the cuff with the folded edge will be the outer cuff.

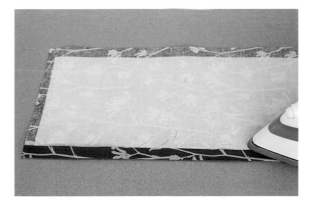

3. Fold each cuff lengthwise, with the right sides of the fabric together. Unfold the seam allowance and align it with the seam allowance on the other side. Stitch the cuff side seams between the folded bottom edge and the creased fold line, backstitching at both ends.

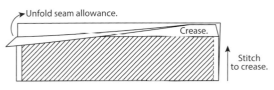

4. Turn the cuff right side out, and with the outer cuff to the wrong side of the sleeve, match the unturned seam allowance to the cuff-line edge of the shirt. Pin the ends of the cuff absolutely flush with the edges of the plackets. Adjust the pleats or gathers, if necessary, to make the sleeve fit exactly to the cuff, pinning it at regular intervals.

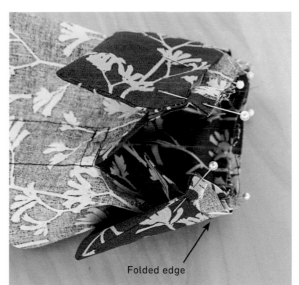

Folded edge

NOTE

The pleats on a sleeve often need adjusting because of the variation in the width of the placket when it is sewn to the sleeve. The extra fabric in the pleat allows for these adjustments to be made at the sewing machine, but it also means that you can change the cuff size of a pattern to fit a smaller or larger wrist without having to alter the sleeve pattern itself.

5. Turn the sleeve right side out and stitch the cuff to the sleeve through 2 layers only, accurately following the seam allowance and backstitching at both ends of the seam. The folded edge of the cuff remains unstitched at this point.

NOTE

On very small garments, it's often easier to do Steps 4 and 5 before Step 3—sewing the unfolded cuff edge to the sleeve, and then folding and stitching the side edges of the cuff. Try both ways and see which works for you.

6. Fold the cuff up over the end of the sleeve, folding the seam allowances into the cuff. Align the folded edges of the turning a generous ¹⁄₁₆″ (2 mm) over the seam and press the cuff into shape, creasing the fold on the outer edge. Use fusible tape, a fabric glue stick, or pins to hold the turning in place.

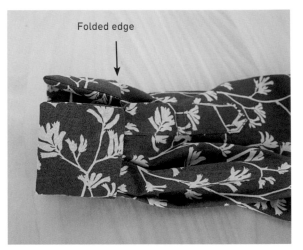

Folded edge

7. Edgestitch the cuff to the sleeve a generous ¹⁄₁₆″ (2 mm) from the fold, and then continue to topstitch around the entire cuff ¹⁄₁₆″–¼″ (2–6 mm) from the edges.

SLEEVE HEMS

Skill Level: Basic to Intermediate

Long sleeves can be converted to short sleeves on most garments with a simple double-turned hem. Sleeves on blouses and dresses can be finished this way or with a bound edge (see Attaching Binding to Seam-Allowance Edges, page 35).

Prepare the Pattern

1. Rule across the sleeve pattern at the level where you would like the new sleeve to finish, and trace a new pattern to this line. Rule a line below this line to mark the hem depth—1″ (2.5 cm) for children's wear or 1¼″ (3.2 cm) for adults—plus ⅜″ (1 cm) for the turning.

2. Fold the pattern along the new sleeve-length line and trace the underarm seamline (and seam allowances) through to the hem. Cut out the pattern; then fold the ⅜″ (1 cm) turning on the bottom edge. Trim off the overhanging edges of the turning.

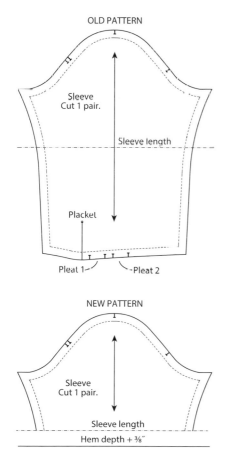

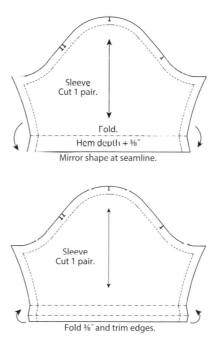

Mirror shape at seamline.

Fold ⅜″ and trim edges.

Sew the Sleeve Hem

1. Sew and finish the underarm seam on the sleeve.

2. Turn and press the ⅜″ (1 cm) turning toward the wrong side of the sleeve; then turn and press the hem in place.

3. Edgestitch the hem to the inside of the sleeve a generous ¹⁄₁₆″ (2 mm) from the turned edge.

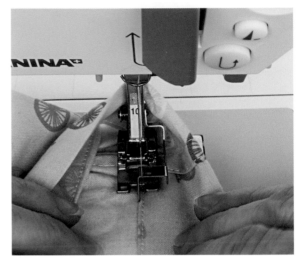

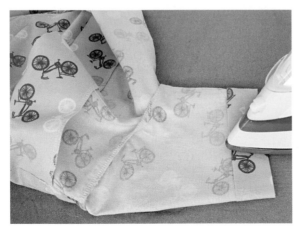

Glossary

BACKSTITCH: A machine stitch that secures the ends of any row of machine stitching with a small reverse stitch. Sew anywhere between two and five stitches forward, then the same in reverse, and finally the same over the top of those stitches. Also called a *backtack* in industrial settings.

BACKTACK: See BACKSTITCH.

BAG OUT: To sew a garment component with right sides together so that when it is turned to the right side all the seam allowances are enclosed (for example, collars and cuffs).

BASTING: A temporary line of stitching used to hold fabric in place during garment construction. It is sewn with the intention of pulling the stitching out after the final seams or topstitching are complete. Basting by hand is usually done with a simple running stitch, and machine basting is done with the largest stitch length setting. Also called *tacking*.

BLOCK: A foundation pattern that is used by pattern makers to develop a new design. It can be a digital file, a paper tracing, or a pattern made on more durable materials, like craft, oaktag, or manila paper. Also called a *sloper*.

BUTTON EXTENSION: On a pattern or draft, the allowance for the fabric that sits underneath and to the outside of the buttons on a garment (see Adding the Button Extension, page 58).

CROTCH SEAM: The seam that joins the two legs of a pair of pants—CF to CB.

DART PICK-UP: The area between the V-shape of the dart stitch lines, which is "taken out" of the garment surface when the dart is sewn.

DRAFT: The plan of a garment pattern design, kept on a separate piece of paper as a saved copy of the design (page 20).

EASING: When one seamline is made slightly longer than the other to allow for extra fullness in part of a garment. Before the seam is sewn, the longer edge is gently squished up on a row of stitches slightly to the inside of the seam allowance until the two garment pieces match together without puckering.

EDGE STITCH: Topstitching that is within $\frac{1}{16}$″–$\frac{1}{8}$″ (2–3 mm) of the edge or seam.

FACING: The fabric support on the inside of an exposed edge of a garment—such as a neckline, waistline, or button opening. It is usually in the same fabric as the garment, with interfacing for extra structure and support.

FELLED SEAM: A seam finish that is often used on men's shirts and jeans. The seam allowances of a $\frac{1}{2}$″ (12 mm) or $\frac{5}{8}$″ (15 mm) seam are folded under and topstitched to the garment, enclosing all the raw edges.

FINISHING: To stop fabric from fraying on exposed seam allowances, the edges are sewn with a serger or zigzag stitch, trimmed with pinking shears, or bound with bias binding.

FRENCH SEAM: A fine finishing technique for seams that is often used on sheer fabrics. With the wrong sides of the fabric together, a narrow seam is sewn. The fabric is then turned so that the right sides are facing, and another seam is sewn, encasing the raw edges of the first seam.

GATHERING: When extra fullness is required, more than for ease, a larger piece of fabric can be drawn in and stitched to a smaller piece. A gathering stitch is made with the largest stitch length in two parallel rows, about $\frac{1}{8}$″ (3 mm) apart, on the seam allowance. Do not back-stitch or cut the threads short. To gather, pull the thread that came from the bobbin, and the fabric will pucker up.

GRAIN OF FABRIC: The direction of the weave in the fabric. Straight grain—the strongest, most stable grain—is parallel to the selvage. The crosswise grain runs between the selvages at a 90° angle from the straight grain. The bias is at a 45° angle from the straight grain, and it is the direction of a woven fabric that has the most drape and stretch.

"GROWN ON": Facings and garment components are joined during the pattern-making stage, eliminating the need for seams.

OVERLOCKER: See SERGER.

PATTERN: A paper or cardboard copy of a garment component that is used for cutting fabric pieces.

PINK: To trim fabric with pinking shears.

PIVOTING: Stitching to a point and then, with the needle down, lifting the presser foot and turning the fabric to align the continuing seam in a new direction.

PLACKET: A finished edge on an opening— usually a separate piece—that is topstitched to the garment at the front of a shirt or above the cuff on a sleeve.

PLEAT: A fold in the fabric that is stitched into a seamline, used to add fullness to an area of a garment.

PROVING: See TRUEING.

RAGLAN SLEEVE: A sleeve style with seams that travel from the neckline to the underarm. Often used on knitwear and sportswear.

RAW EDGE: The cut edge of fabric that is not enclosed in a seam.

SELF FABRIC: The main fabric of a garment—not the lining.

SERGER: A specialized sewing machine that uses three, four, or five threads that interloop in a neat stitch formation. It trims and sews an edge on seam allowances to stop the fabric from fraying; it is also used to seam knit fabrics. Also called an overlocker.

SLASH AND OPEN/CLOSE: A pattern-making alteration made by opening or closing areas of the pattern to add or remove fullness.

SLOPER: See BLOCK.

STAY STITCH: Stitching used to stabilize cut garment pieces around curved edges, such as necklines and waistlines, so that the fabric does not distort or stretch during garment construction. The stitches stay in place even after the final seams are sewn, so stay stitching is sewn on the seam allowance side of the seamline and is not visible on the outside of the garment.

STITCH-IN-THE-DITCH: Used to discreetly top-stitch one layer of fabric to another when there is a seam on the upper piece. Align the needle and topstitch directly into the deepest part (the "ditch") where two fabrics join in a seam.

TACKING: See BASTING.

TOP STITCH: Stitching that is done from the right side of the garment. It can be decorative, creating contrast and definition along seams, or structural, holding patch pockets in place and so on.

TRUEING: Neatening the lines on a pattern and checking that matching lines are the same length. Also called proving.

UNDERSTITCH: An edge stitch used to create a clean fold line back from a seamed edge. The seam allowance is sewn 1/16"–1/8" (2–3 mm) from the seam on the right side of the fabric, catching all the seam allowances on the underside.

ZIPPER CHAIN: The line of "teeth" on the zipper.

Index

Resources

Fabric

There's nothing like shopping for fabrics in person. But if you're looking for any of the fabrics used to make the garments in this book, they were manufactured by the following companies:

CLOUD9 FABRICS   cloud9fabrics.com

FREESPIRIT FABRIC   freespiritfabrics.com

MICHAEL MILLER FABRICS   michaelmillerfabrics.com

Fusible Tape

Vliesofix/Bondaweb T6 is my preferred fusible tape, but it can be tricky to find in some regions. Do an Internet search for the product to find suppliers in your country. Alternatively, use Steam-A-Seam 2 tape.

Glue-Stick Pens

SEWLINE   sewline-products.com

Pattern-Making and Tailoring Supplies

ACESEWING.COM (U.S.)   acesewing.com

B. BLACK & SONS (U.S.)   bblackandsons.com

MORPLAN (UK)   www.morplan.com

M. RECHT ACCESSORIES (AUSTRALIA / NEW ZEALAND)   mrecht.com.au

RICHARD THE THREAD (U.S.)   richardthethread.com

WAWAK SEWING (U.S.)   wawak.com

Further Reading

SEWING BASICS

The BurdaStyle Sewing Handbook, by Nora Abousteit and Alison Kelly (Potter Craft)

The Colette Sewing Handbook, by Sarai Mitnick (Krause Publications)

Sew U, by Wendy Mullin and Eviana Hartman (Bulfinch Press)

FITTING AND ADVANCED PATTERN MAKING

Fitting and Pattern Alteration, by Elizabeth Liechty, Judith Rasband, and Della Pottberg-Steineckert (Fairchild Books)

Patternmaking for Fashion Design, by Helen Joseph-Armstrong (Harper & Rowe Publishing; Pearson)*

The Perfect Fit: The Classic Guide to Altering Patterns, by the Editors of Creative Publishing (Creative Publishing International)

Pattern-making books by Winifred Aldrich are a good visual resource for creating more complex designs.

Note: There are many editions of this text, and they are all good.

SEWING TIPS AND TRICKS

PatternReview.com 1,000 Clever Sewing Shortcuts and Tips, by Deepika Prakash (Creative Publishing International)

You Sew, Girl!, by Nicole Mallalieu (ABC Books)

Read anything by Claire Shaeffer, Sandra Betzina, Nancy Zieman, *Threads* magazine ... really any book about dressmaking that you can find. There is *always* something to learn!